Patrick Walsh Press, publishers
2206 S. Priest Suite 105
Tempe, Arizona 85282

SINDON

A LAYMAN'S GUIDE TO
THE SHROUD OF TURIN

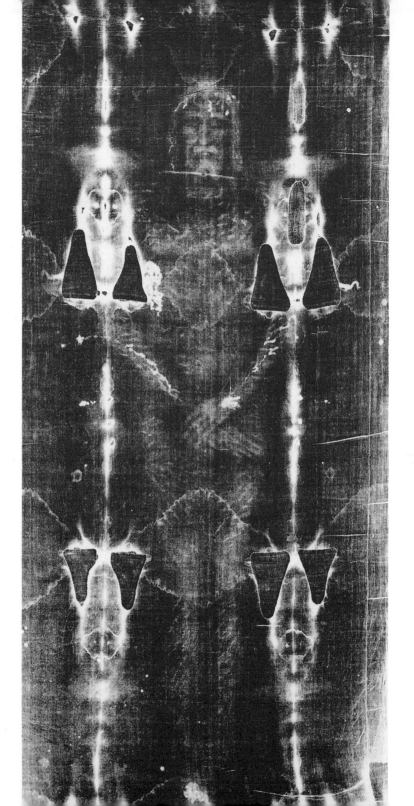

SINDON

A LAYMAN'S GUIDE TO THE SHROUD OF TURIN

FRANK O. ADAMS

CONTRIBUTING SCIENCE EDITOR
JOHN A. DeSALVO, Ph.D.

SYNERGY BOOKS

Library of Congress Cataloging in Publication Data

Adams, Frank O., 1905 -
   Sindon: A Layman's Guide to the Shroud of Turin.

   Bibliography: p.
   Includes index.
   1. Holy Shroud. I. DeSalvo, John A. II. Title.
BT587.S4A3 1982   232.9'66   82-90138

ISBN 0-86700-008-2
ISBN 0-86700-009-0   (pbk.)

Photo Credits:
1, 2, 3, 4, 6, 8, 10, 11, 12, 13, 14, 15, 16, 17, 18, 19, 20, 21, 22, 23, 24, 25, 26
   courtesy of the Holy Shroud Guild.
32, 32A courtesty of John A. DeSalvo, Ph.D.
28 courtesy of Francis L. Filas, S.J.
29 copyright © Vernon Miller, Brooks Institute of Photography, Santa Barbara.
Frontispiece, 5, 27, 30, 31 copyright © Barrie M. Schwortz, Santa Barbara.

ABOUT THE AUTHOR

Since his retirement in 1960 from the United States
Army, Col. Frank O. Adams has devoted his time and
energy to a non-profit foundation, and to his extensive
research into the Shroud of Turin. In the course of his
travels, he has given hundreds of lectures on the historical,
religious and scientific background of the Shroud, and he
continues to research its history and the arguments for its
authenticity as the burial shroud of Jesus Christ.

Sindon: A Layman's Guide To The Shroud of Turin, is his second
book on the Shroud. His first volume, *A Scientific Search for the
Face of Jesus,* was published in 1972 and included an evidential
portrait of Jesus based on The Shroud of Turin. *Sindon*
updates his previous exhaustive study of the Shroud of
Turin, and adds a summary, and implications of the latest
research results.

DEDICATION

For the late Helen Adelaide Ellsworth van Loben Sels whose
awareness, love and prayers made my first vision possible.
This overcame my agnosticism and led me to His works.
And Rev. Allan Barham B.D. who in introducing me to the
Shroud of Turin provided a basis for my beliefs
to become knowledge.

TABLE OF CONTENTS

	Acknowledgments	xi
	A Word From The Author	1
1	The Shroud Of Turin	5
2	Conjectured Early Background of the Shroud	11
3	The Image Of Edessa	21
4	Wilson's Theory Of The Shroud After Constantinople	28
5	Other Theories Of The Shroud's History	37
6	Photography Reveals A Mystery	47
7	Vignon's Research	58
8	Barbet & His Medical Research	66
9	The Age Of The Shroud And Where It Has Been	82
10	Other Modern Scientific Research Of The Shroud	92
11	The New London Symposium	98
12	Personal Reflections On The Resurrection	117
	Chronology of the Shroud	133
	Bibliography	137
	Index	141

ACKNOWLEDGMENTS

My deepest appreciation is expressed to the authors listed in the Bibliography with full understanding that a large portion of my efforts constitute only an analytical review of their major contributions to Mankind's knowledge of the Holy Shroud of Turin.

Much gratitude is felt for the warmth of the courtesy and consideration displayed by the Rev. Adam J. Otterbein, C.ss.R., and the Rev. Peter M. Rinaldi, S.D.B., not only for their permission to use the copyrighted pictures of the Holy Shroud, but for valuable assistance and suggestions dealing with major portions of my manuscript.

A heart-felt "well done" to Susy Smith who was commissioned to give me literary assistance. She relieved me of a great deal of writing and research which physical problems have made arduous and painful for me. In addition she learned to use a word processor for the project. She cheerfully and enthusiastically gave of her extensive experience based on her authorship of twenty-eight books.

Thanks are due as well to Barrie Schwortz, a member of the Brooks Institute of Photography faculty, who was official photographer during the STURP researches in Turin, who provided many of the photographs reproduced in this work.

Much appreciation, also, to my publisher for the courtesy and consideration I have been shown. To Rosemary Walsh, who graciously and helpfully performed miracles on a computer, as well as providing helpful comments. And to Kenneth L. Bacher, my principal editor. His suggestions improved my manuscript without ever attempting to make it his book.

I am grateful to Dorothy Cirpino whose fluency in French and Italian and gracious cooperation provided otherwise unavailable material.

My special thanks to those who aided and cooperated in so many ways; the late Jeffrey Furst; Mary and Herbert DeLoria; John Bulla; Edith J. Fraser; James McBain; Josephine and Richard Jepperson; Roger E. Braden; and my helpmate, Dorothy, who contributed worthwhile ideas, valuable constructive criticism, a superb job of editing, and manifested a high degree of patience with the birth pangs attendant upon this endeavor.

A WORD FROM THE AUTHOR

S INDON (SYN-DON) is the Greek word for a burial shroud. From it, the term sindonology has been coined to describe the study of the winding sheet now known as the Shroud of Turin, which many believe to be the burial cloth of Jesus Christ.

Those who are doing this research are called sindonologists. Under that name, hundreds of scientists and students have dedicated their efforts to try to determine the Shroud of Turin's age, how the manifestation occurred on the cloth, and whether or not it could be a forgery. Also, finally, to determine if there is any way to prove scientifically the possibility that it is actually the Shroud of Jesus Christ.

I became a sindonologist in May of 1966. I had given a talk on meditation for a spiritual study group at Willoughby Vicarage in Warwickshire, England. The leader of the group, and my host, was the Reverend Mr. Allan Barham, a Church of England (Episcopal) minister. The following morning we went into his study for a chat. On the wall was a framed photograph of the Holy Shroud of Turin.

"What is that?" I asked him.

He teased me, "You mean with all you know of theology, church history, and the Bible, you don't know anything about the Shroud?"

1

I had to reply in the negative. He then showed me slides of this length of cloth that purportedly wrapped the body of Jesus of Nazareth after the crucifixion, on which are pale brownish-yellow stains that depict the front and back of a crucified man. At the conclusion of Allan's short talk that accompanied the pictures, I told him, "I have to have a set of those slides. Where do I get them?"

He smiled. "Well," he said, "it just happens that I have an extra set." So when I caught the train to London later that day, a new treasure went with me: my first set of slides of the Shroud of Turin.

I immediately commenced an intensive study of everything that had been written in English about this unique and challenging relic. At the conclusion of my initial careful examination of all the available facts, I was convinced that the burial cloth had wrapped Jesus. Feeling an acute desire to share my strong belief with others, I began seeking speaking engagements with any church or group which wished to share my knowledge. I have now given more than five hundred talks on this subject.

Very early some of my listeners challenged me with the question, "Assuming your conclusions are correct, what is the Shroud's importance?"

After carefully evaluating this point, it appeared to me that one of the greatest benefits was the possibility that a true likeness could be developed from the dimensions of the face of Jesus on this cloth. Through the centuries artists have created tens of thousands of icons, paintings, mosaics and carvings, all based solely on Christian piety, imagination and guesswork. These, of course, reflect a deep yearning on the part of humankind to know what Christ looked like. And so I decided to attempt to have such a portrait created, based on the evidence, of the Shroud. In 1970, this was done.

Since then, I have been frequently asked, "What is so important about His appearance?"

The logical answer was that most human beings like to have pictures of those they love. So a demand for an evidential portrait of Jesus is very understandable.

In the question period after one of my lectures, author Helen Reeves said, "Colonel Adams, you have given us more facts and detail than anyone could possibly remember: your talk is all meat and no potatoes. Why don't you develop and pass out fact sheets at your lectures that we can take home and refer to?"

The only means of adequately meeting this request was to write a book, so I did. All rights to *A Scientific Search For The Face Of Jesus*, published in 1972 (now out-of-print), and the copyrighted portrait were assigned to a non-profit foundation.

Since 1972, a wealth of research has added much additional knowledge about the Shroud. Experts in many scientific disciplines have actually handled this cloth and subjected it to the "seeking fingers" of modern scientific equipment. Their findings are reported in various sources, but it is time now for a fresh evaluation of the pros and cons.

My purpose in writing this book on the Shroud of Turin is twofold, since the evidence has convinced me that it is the burial cloth that wrapped Jesus in the tomb: First of all, to present to the general public, in layman's language, the scientific, artistic, theological and historical research. Secondly, to present strong support for belief in the Resurrection; grounds for credence in an often skeptical, scientific, materialistic culture.

Dr. John DeSalvo is a biophysicist, physiology professor, and Director of the Basic Science Division at Northwestern College of Chiropractic in St. Paul, Minnesota. He lectures extensively nationwide on the Shroud of Turin, and he has concentrated his studies of the Shroud on theories relating to the image formation process.

In addition to his research and teaching, Dr. DeSalvo reviewed the text of *Sindon: "A Layman's Guide to the Shroud of Turin"* to insure the accuracy of the scientific information included. He contributed much scientific information, including his own theory of the image formation process, which postulates that the image was formed by lactic acid contained in the perspiration of the man on the Shroud. Dr. DeSalvo's hypothesis appears for the first time in Chapter 11.

Frank O. Adams
Tucson, Arizona
April, 1982

1

THE SHROUD OF TURIN

A GREAT NUMBER OF SCIENTISTS, laymen and churchmen of all denominations now believe that the winding sheet in which Christ was wrapped in the sepulcher is actually in existence and located in Turin (Torino), Italy. It is known as the Shroud of Turin (Plate No. 1). It is the most sacred, the most controversial, and perhaps even the most important relic in all Christendom.

The Shroud itself is of impressive dimensions— fourteen feet, three inches long and three feet, seven inches wide. It is a single piece of time-faded linen with a strip approximately three and one-half inches wide running the length of the left-hand side. Only one seam was used for this attachment. On this sheet is an image which is so faint it looks more like a shadow cast on the cloth. The figure is the pale imprint in a honey-straw color (except for the blood stains, which are a deep burgundy) of the front and back of a powerfully-built man with a beard and long hair, between five feet seven inches and six feet tall, weighing between 155 and 175 pounds, and laid out in the normal position employed in Jewish burials of the First Century. Excavation of graves in the Qumran community by the shores of the Dead Sea revealed skeletons on their

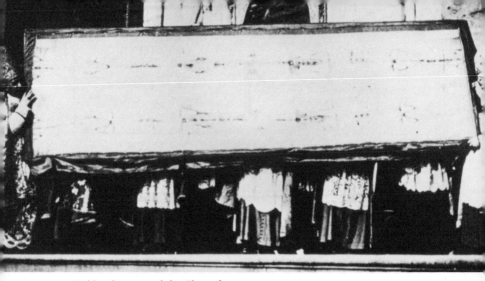

1. Public showing of the Shroud in 1933.

backs with hands crossed over their groins, just as is depicted by the image on the Shroud, but no other winding sheet presumably dating from that period has ever been found.

Even before one's eyes focus on the figure stretching down the middle of the cloth, they are drawn to a twin line of scars that dominate it—a number of patches which look somewhat like long spears running symmetrically up and down the linen on each side of the body image. These are repairs from a fire which almost destroyed the Shroud in the Sixteenth Century. Over the worst of the damage the Poor Clares, a religious order of nuns founded by St. Clare, sewed fourteen large triangular-shaped patches and eight small ones, all made from altar cloth.

The Shroud reposes in the Royal Chapel of the House of Savoy, where it has been for centuries, except during World War II, when it was removed to Avellino for safety. This spectacular edifice, circular in shape and faced with black marble, is part of Turin's Cathedral of St. John the Baptist (Duomo Giovanni Battista), which adjoins the royal palace. Plate No. 2 shows the front of this cathedral. In the background, on the right-hand side, one can see the spire of the cupola of the Royal Chapel.

Through the centuries, humankind has demonstrated an awed reverence for God in the manner in which it has built its places of worship. The home of the Holy Shroud is no exception to this general rule. The Cathedral of St. John was erected more than four hundred years ago. The greatest art and architecture available at that time were included in its construction.

For the Shroud's protection, numerous safeguards have been taken. The Shroud is rolled around a velvet-covered staff, which in turn is wrapped in red silk. It lies in a four-foot-long wooden casket ornamented with silver emblems

2. The Cathedral of St. John in Turin.

3. The Shroud of Turin's Silver Casket.

of the Passion. (Plate No. 3). This casket is kept in an asbestos-wrapped iron chest and sealed with three locks, each requiring a separate key. The iron chest reposes within a wooden box. The painted cover of this wooden box is all that is visible through the two iron grilles in the upper receptacle of the altar in which the Shroud is stored in the Royal Chapel. (Plate No. 4).

The only thing known for certain about the history of the Shroud is that in about 1353 it was in the possession of a family known as de Charny (or de Charney) in Lirey, France. Prior to that time, its whereabouts cannot be verified; any possible prior locations or movements lie hidden in past centuries. There are conjectures, of course, now pretty well disproved, that it actually began its existence in Lirey, the product of some ingenious artistic forger. Wherever it came from, it is now owned by Umberto (Humbert) II of Savoy, the exiled king of Italy, although for centuries it has been in the custody of the Archdiocese of Turin. For its protection, the House of Savoy and its advisers in the church allow it to be shown on rare occasions, and great masses of people assemble in Turin at such times. Not until 1969 were scientific investigators allowed to spend any time examining it. Since then some of the most modern techniques have been used in efforts to determine its authenticity.

As Kenneth Weaver says in a story entitled, "The Mystery of the Shroud" in the *National Geographic*:

> The curious blend of history and legend behind that story glitters with kings and dukes, crusaders and popes, and perhaps a consummately clever charlatan. The modern detectives probing the mystery include art historians, pathologists, linguists, biblical scholars, textile experts, chemists, physicists, and photographic specialists.

This list can now include botanists and criminologists as well.

4. The Altar in the Royal Chapel where the Shroud is kept.

Possibly the most exciting development in the study of the Shroud occurred when it was first photographed in 1898 by an Italian photographer named Secondo Pia, and it was discovered that the figure on the cloth is actually a negative. Photography, either color or black and white, and even television, seems to intensify the image. The image is then more apparent than it is to the naked eye, for under ordinary circumstances it is extremely difficult to distinguish, except when viewed from a distance of several feet.

John Walsh writes in his book, *The Shroud*:

> Today the Shroud of Turin, in terms of the number of people involved, the time and effort given to it, and the size of its literature, has become one of the two or three most celebrated 'mysteries' of all time. In a popular, purely secular sense, it ranks with the question of the Shakespeare authorship and the legend of Atlantis.

Walsh's book was written in 1963. How much more of a mystery the Shroud has now become since science has recently declared it not to be a forgery!

No one has yet been able to totally prove that the Shroud of Turin is actually the winding sheet of Jesus of Nazareth. The account of the search that has been undertaken by so many to prove its authenticity is a detective story unequalled in history. It will give us provocative and challenging new perspectives as we attempt to unravel this great mystery.

CONJECTURED
EARLY BACKGROUND
OF THE SHROUD

EFORE THE APPEARANCE of the Shroud in Lirey, France, in the mid-Fourteenth Century, nothing is known for certain as to its whereabouts. There are various reports of sightings of a shroud from time to time and place to place, but nothing that can be substantiated in any way.

Because it is presumed by so many to be the actual winding sheet in which Jesus was wrapped, any search that might be made for historical data to give us clues may well begin with the circumstances surrounding the crucifixion and what happened immediately thereafter.

Interestingly enough, Paul Vignon, who was the first scientist to study the Shroud seriously, said in 1902 in his book *The Shroud of Christ*, "We shall find that accounts given in the Gospels agree absolutely with our scientific observations."

The narrative in the scriptural report, however, is somewhat meager. There are very brief statements in the four Gospels concerning the circumstances immediately following the crucifixion. This is further complicated by the question of the original language of the biblical text: scholars dispute whether it was Hebrew or Aramaic. However, it is agreed that Jesus and His followers spoke the latter, although they must have also known Hebrew.

There were no recording devices, of course, but it is not difficult to imagine an inspired listener at one of the Great Teacher's discourses hurrying afterward to a scribe and dictating some sayings or a parable. It has been suggested that such incidents resulted in a wealth of treasured scrolls that later were used in the compiling of the Gospels.

Whether written in Aramaic or Hebrew, they were soon translated into Greek as the faith spread eastward and westward from Palestine. At first, the proliferation eastward was greater, reaching even China and India.

Today, the Holy Apostolic and Catholic Church of the East takes a fixed position that "they received their scriptures from the hands of the blessed Apostles themselves, in the Aramaic original." They claim their bible, the *Peshitta*, stems from the beginnings of Christianity and has not been changed or revised in any way.

The following, are extracts from the English translation of the Greek version as contained in the Revised Standard Edition:

> When the even was come there came a rich man of Arimathea, named Joseph, who also was a disciple of Jesus. He went to Pilate and asked for the body of Jesus. Then Pilate ordered it to be given to him. And Joseph took the body, and wrapped it in a clean linen shroud, and laid it in his own new tomb, which he had hewn in the rock; and he rolled a great stone to the door of the tomb and departed (Matt. 27:57ff).

St. Mark's account reads,

> And he brought a linen, and taking Him down, wrapped Him in the linen shroud, and laid Him in a tomb which had been hewn out of the rock; and he rolled a stone against the door of the tomb (Mark 15:46).

In the Greek, the word *sindon* is used in both these excerpts, and the same word also appears in St. Luke's account,

> Then he took Him down and wrapped Him in a linen shroud and laid Him in a rock-hewn tomb, where no one had ever yet been laid (Luke 23:53).

Those three accounts agree with each other, even though purportedly they were compiled in different places from the oral tradition handed down from witnesses. Obviously, the corpse was wrapped in a linen cloth of thin material, sufficiently large to envelop the body, for that is what a *sindon* is.

Plate No. 5 shows an oil painting from the Sixteenth Century, attributed to Giulio Clovio, a disciple of Rafael. The top shows the first known painting of the Shroud of Turin. It is held out to its full length by three angels, revealing both the front and back reliefs. The lower portion indicates the manner in which the man on the Shroud was placed between two halves of the burial cloth.

St. John adds further information. After speaking of the intervention of Joseph of Arimathea, he says,

> Nicodemus also, who had at first come to him by night, came bringing a mixture of myrrh and aloes, about a hundred pounds' weight (John 19:39).

This quantity as expressed in Greek would constitute seventy pounds today. These men came with the intention of burying Jesus according to the Jewish custom. If they could have immediately proceeded to complete the final rites, they would have carefully taken several ritualistic

5. 16th Century oil painting, attributed to Guilio Clovio showing the Shroud. *(Barrie M. Schwortz)*

steps of washing and anointing, and finally, they would have enveloped the body in the winding sheet that the first three Gospels mention.

But these operations were lengthy and could not be done quickly, and it was already late in the day. Moreover, it was Friday, when all work was forbidden after sundown. The first three stars appearing in the heavens signaled the beginning of the Sabbath, and that particular Sabbath was doubly sacred because it was also Passover, the most solemn feast of the year. It is therefore certain that Joseph of Arimathea and Nicodemus would not have had time to prepare the body in the usual manner for burial. They did what they could in the limited time at their disposal, but they certainly would have had to postpone the completion of the unfinished obsequies until the day after the Sabbath.

On the morning of the first Easter, we learn from St. John, he and Peter found the empty tomb and the "burial cloths."

Now we have to consider what such conscientious Jews would have done under these circumstances. The law said they should not have anything to do with garments that had been on a dead body, even presumably one that had risen from the dead and disappeared out of a sealed sepulcher. Such linens, cloths and garments had to be handled with tongs and then burned. If burial garments touched a practicing Jew, he would have to go through the purification rites as outlined in the Torah.

Perhaps they believed that they were not breaking the law, that Jesus was not dead but had resurrected. Their subsequent acts demonstrated the extent of this conviction. Under these circumstances, it is very unlikely that they would have destroyed the linen cloth that wrapped Him. Logically, such an object would have become the most precious of precious reminders of the man they loved; something they would have treasured and safely stored.

Shortly thereafter, the persecution of the Christians commenced, first under the dedicated leadership of Saul of Tarsus and others who succeeded him, and later by the Romans as exemplified by Nero. If such a burial cloth were saved and treasured, it would certainly have been hidden carefully at least until the persecutions abated. John could have rescued it and given it to Mary, the mother of Jesus, just as today it is customary to take the flag off the coffin of a military man and give it to the bereaved wife or parent.

It would be doubtful that Mary could have kept it for long, however, for there had to be a frantic furor among the leaders of the Sanhedrin. The teachings of the bold apostles and their claim of a resurrection must have caused consternation among the temple leaders so that they would have done anything within their power to find such a convincing piece of evidence as the Shroud and destroy it. It would therefore have been practical to turn it over for safe-keeping to one of the Nazarene's Roman followers, who as a citizen had the power of the legions to protect his property and possessions.

When the times became less turbulent, probably thirty or thirty-five years later, it could have been brought out of hiding and occasionally displayed to trusted believers. Some centuries later there may even have been a monastery erected to house this relic somewhere close to Jerusalem, perhaps near the Jordan where John the Baptist baptized Jesus. This conjecture would fit the stories that have come down to us.

All reference to a shroud disappeared from written history for centuries. Then it gradually began to be reported as existing, and having been seen. The first account could be a legend, preserved by Nicephorus. This story says that the lady who was beatified as St. Helena was shown a shroud in Jerusalem during the Fourth Century.

Next, we have the report of a pilgrim in 570 who returned from Jerusalem and talked of a shroud that was kept in a monastery beside the Jordan. A little over half a century later, St. Braulion said he believed in the authenticity of a "winding sheet in which our Lord was wrapped."

There are other reports scattered through the centuries like tiny pinpoints of light. The earliest reference listed in the *New Catholic Encyclopedia* is St. Nino in the Fifth or Sixth Century; and Antonius Placentinus can also be cited for the same period. In 670, a French bishop named Arculph reported having seen and kissed the Shroud, and as the years rolled by, other men also spoke of it. Among these were the English theologian, the Venerable Bede, who is buried in Durham Cathedral in England, and the Emperor Baldwin. St. John Damascene mentions the *sindon* as being among the relics venerated by the Christians, and St. Willibald spoke of seeing a shroud in the neighborhood of Jerusalem. Then there is the song of the voyage of Charlemagne to Jerusalem. This mentions the *sindon* Jesus wore "when He was laid and stretched in the tomb."

There are a few others including a letter of the Twelfth Century historian, William of Tyre, which refers specifically to "a shroud of Christ." There is also a letter of Alexius of Comenos, some documents of Peter the Deacon, and two catalogues made by pilgrims to Constantinople. There are less than twenty of these random reports from antique texts, stretching over a period of 700 years. They may all be apocryphal, or any one of them may be true.

Of one thing one may be confident, however; that from the time of the Roman Emperor Constantine, there was a big change in Christianity. Early in the Fourth Century, Constantine Augustus, called the Great, is reported to have seen a cross in the sky and to have been converted. He made Christianity the official religion of Rome, and permitted harsh persecution of those who practiced pagan rites.

His nephew, Julian, termed the Apostate because he was non-Christian and allowed all to worship as they chose, succeeded to the throne in 360 and died in battle three years later. Despite the fact that Julian had shown tolerance to all faiths, he left an empire torn by strong divisive feelings on religious questions. Only in an isolated corner of the empire such as Judea would it have been safe to display a Christian relic in those troubled times.

During this period of change there were also alterations in the way Christ was pictured in all reproductions of Him. It seemed as if no one had known what He really looked like before that time, but that they did after the end of the period of persecution of the Christians. This may indicate that the custodians of this burial cloth now felt that they could safely show it to many people, instead of secretly to a few important and favored individuals.

It is a fact known to historians of art that the physical appearance of Christ in paintings, sculptures and carvings is rather sharply divided into two periods, with the line of demarcation running through the Fourth Century. In the first period, from the evidence of the catacomb pictures and some early Christian sarcophagi, Christ is depicted as an Apollo-like beardless youth with an oval, innocent face. In none of the art that has been preserved from the first three hundred years after His death is He seen any other way. Then, with the emergence of Christianity under Constantine, this obviously symbolic portrayal was discarded and pictures of Christ began to appear quite differently. Now He consistently resembled the face we see on the Shroud of Turin.

Many pictures and icons of this period exist today, coming from Russia, Greece, Egypt, the Balkans and Italy. In all of them, there are many significantly similar features: the mustache and forked beard, hair parted in the middle and falling to the shoulders. These were distinctive characteristics of the Nazarenes. In addition, there were the three-sided square between the brows, the second V above this, the transverse streak across the forehead, the accentuated cheeks and enlarged left nostril. The heavily drawn owlish eyes which were also evident in most of the reproductions could today be explained by the fact that the Shroud image is a negative, and what is seen is the outline of the eye socket. (Plate No. 6 gives an excellent example of this type of portraiture.)

6. Portrait of Jesus in the Roman Catacombs from the 6th Century.

Paul Vignon, the foremost early researcher into the authenticity of the Shroud of Turin, is the one who conceived the idea that these numerous icons and portraits had somehow been based on the face of the Shroud. Checking them in the museums and libraries of Paris, he discovered dramatic evidence that there was more than a casual link between them. Of the hundreds of Byzantine icons he examined, eighty percent had the identifying mark between the eyes as well as many other points of similarity. The earliest icons he found with sindonlike similarities were copies of what was known as the "Image of Edessa," of which more will be said in the next chapter.

Vignon wrote in a 1937 magazine,

> There are many representations of Christ, notably the Image of Edessa, which could be derived only from the Shroud. A careful study of these copies, which I recently completed, shows that the . . . face visible on the Shroud served as a model for artists as early as the fifth century. The artists did not copy slavishly, but tried to interpret the face, translating the masklike features into a living portrait, which was still a recognizable copy of the original.

Vignon noticed that the very oddities of the Shroud, certain peculiarities that were really accidental imperfections in the image or the fabric itself, were reproduced, appearing again and again in a whole series of ancient art works, even though artistically they made no sense. Surely, this could mean only one thing, he decided; ancient artists had taken their conception of a bearded, long-haired man from the image on the Shroud, and had included the anomalies which were aspects of the negative image because of a feeling that they were in some mysterious way connected with the earthly appearance of Jesus.

3

THE IMAGE OF EDESSA

I F IT WERE TRUE THAT THE SHROUD had been
hidden during this time, where had it been? Of course,
no one knows for sure. But Ian Wilson, secretary of the
British Society for the Turin Shroud, has offered in his
book, *The Shroud of Turin*, an hypothesis that has captured
the imagination of many other authors and sindonologists.
Some of this hypothesis is conjecture from legend and art,
he admits, but its parts are worked into a framework based
on fact.

As Wilson researched old papers and letters involving the
period of time from Christ's death to the 1350s when the
Shroud surfaced in Lirey, France, he was led back again and
again to a relic known as the Mandylion. (The word
Mandylion is Greek for cloth or veil.) This was also referred
to as the "Image of Edessa."

It was claimed that the Mandylion was the face of Christ
on a cloth or towel, and its supernatural quality was
recognized early, for it was declared by several sources as
"Not made by hand." Pope Pius, in the 1930s, spoke
similarly of the Shroud of Turin as, "certainly not by the
hand of Man." Descriptions of the Mandylion face were
consistently similar to that of the Shroud in reference to its
watery and blurry character, as well as to its colors, which

were virtually identical to the coloring of the image on the Shroud.

Still, Wilson writes,

> The only reasonable grounds for suggesting common identity were the shared concept of the image having been 'impressed' in some extraordinary manner upon the cloth, and the strangely familiar Shroud-like look of the face on artists' copies of the Mandylion.

However, he adds,

> The most pertinent example of all of the Mandylion's image being identical to that of the Shroud belongs to the earliest firsthand account that we have of any 'viewing' of the Mandylion in Byzantine times—that of the evening of August 15, 944, when the cloth first arrived in Constantinople when . . . two somewhat ignorant sons of the reigning emperor, Romanus Lecapenus, were present.

These young men are reported to have found the Mandylion disappointing because they were unable to distinguish Christ's features clearly, finding the image extremely blurred. "One could only interpret this as a classic reaction of anyone seeing the Shroud for the first time," says Wilson.

Whoever made the Mandylion copies also appears to have been working from the Shroud. "This raises the inevitable question, were Mandylion and Shroud actually one and the same thing?" Wilson asks.

One of the most important documentary sources for the Mandylion's character and history is *The Story of the Image of Edessa.* This was written in the Tenth Century by Constantine Porphyrogenitus, an unknown author especially commissioned by the Emperor, and who was present at the court of Constantinople at the time the Mandylion arrived in the city. Asked to set down all that was known of the cloth to that date, he was probably allowed a special viewing. If not, he certainly gleaned the pertinent details from those who had. This Greek writer, in attempting to surmise how the image had appeared on the cloth, suggested that it was formed during Jesus' agony in the Garden of Gethsemane when "sweat dropped from him like drops of blood" (Luke 22:44).

In his report, Porphyrogenitus said,

> Then they say he took this piece of cloth which we see now . . . and wiped off the drops of bloodlike sweat on it. At once the still-visible impression of that divine face was produced.

Another version suggests that Jesus had asked to wash Himself, and then imprinted His likeness on the linen towel.

There were other theories at that time as to how the face had been formed, all indicating that it came directly from Jesus' contact with the cloth. None, however, implied it was His shroud, because at that time no one thought the Mandylion contained anything more than a face. Wilson suggests this was because it had been folded into four parts. In fact, one of the sources describing this white (or natural color) "towel" used a strange word in the original text, the literal meaning of which is "doubled in four."

The Shroud of Turin as it exists is a sheet of white (or natural color—though now discolored by time) linen about as long as two tablecloths stretched end to end, bearing the imprint of the front and back of a human body. How did the Mandylion come to be folded into four parts, thus revealing only the face? To understand Wilson's surmise about this question, one must understand Edessa at a time shortly after the Crucifixion.

Edessa is the present day bustling, thoroughly Moslem,

town of Urfa in eastern Turkey near the Syrian border. After a rather bad start when the Christian population was almost wiped out, it became for some centuries one of the famed cities of Christendom, having some 300 churches and monasteries. Part of our history of it is semi-legendary, but the archon, or ruler of this city state, Abgar V, is a definite historical personage.

As early as the first century A.D. the image of Christ on a cloth is supposed to have been sent to this monarch to cure him of a disease—the cloth having been brought from Palestine by an evangelist named Thaddeus. The cloth not only healed Abgar, and possibly converted him, but it also converted many of the citizens to Christianity. However, one of his successors was less kindly disposed toward Christianity, and about A.D. 57 a time of religous persecution occurred during which the infant Christian community there was temporarily wiped out.

This revered cloth that King Abgar had received from Palestine had to be hidden. According to Wilson's interpretation of Constantine Porphyrogenitus' account, it was doubled into four, with the head of Christ appearing on the uppermost section, then stretched on a sturdy, box-like frame with fringe around it. Then all but the face was covered with a rich embellishment of gold in what might be called a kind of trellis pattern. The way the whole thing was designed would have made it quite impossible to gain access to the areas of cloth bearing the image of the body without dismantling the entire Mandylion.

Wilson writes:

> At last one arrives at what ostensibly seems to be the explanation of why the Shroud might have gone unrecorded in history—for the completely unforseeable reason that no one at the time recognized it as a shroud.

After this elaborate "picture" was made out of the long piece of cloth which was the Shroud, it was, according to *The Story of the Image of Edessa*, hidden in a space above one of the city gates and carefully bricked up for concealment. There it was to remain, unknown and untouched, for nearly five centuries. By the year 525, Edessa was part of the Byzantine Empire. At that time there was another of the many terrible floods that frequently occurred in that area. The gateway was destroyed, and in its ruins the Mandylion was found.

The Christians of Edessa received it with open arms and cherished it, building a new cathedral to house it—the Hagia Sophia—which was declared to be one of the wonders of the world. But no one ever suspected the existence of the full-length figure of Christ that had for all that time lay hidden in the Mandylion's folds. For centuries it was displayed at the cathedral, and the face was copied widely and sent throughout Christendom.

In the early 940s, the Byzantine Emperor Romanus Lecapenus celebrated his seventieth birthday and did some soul-searching about his life and his accomplishments. He reflected on the fact that the Mandylion, the greatest of all Christian relics at the time, lay hundreds of miles away in Moslem territory. So he sent his most able general to get it; and after several battles, it was procured. In 944, The Mandylion arrived in Constantinople, a glorious new possession for the emperor. There it was highly venerated and closely guarded, as it had been in the recent past.

But it was there in Constantinople that something new appears to have been added to the relic. Someone, or some group, apparently took the Mandylion apart, undid the golden trelliswork, and untwined the fringe from the nails. When they unfolded the cloth, they were no doubt startled to see the concealed full-length figure. Frustratingly, this is another of those moments in the Mandylion's history that has gone unrecorded. There is, therefore, no means of verifying it. However, the story is attested to as a real happening "in an impressive array of circumstantial evidence," said Ian Wilson, when he addressed the 1981 Symposium of the Shroud of Turin Research Project.

The first indications that the entire Shroud was now revealed come from Western sources. Datable to sometime before 1130, is an interpolation in an original Eighth-Century sermon by Pope Stephen III, which, referring to the Mandylion, tells us:

> For the very same mediator between God and man [Christ], that he might in every way satisfy the king [Abgar], stretched his whole body on a cloth, white as snow, on which the glorious image of the Lord's face and the length of his whole body was so divinely transformed that it was sufficient for those who could not see the Lord bodily in the flesh, to see the transfiguration made on the cloth.

The History of the Church written by the English monk, Ordericus Vitalis, about 1130, stated:

> Abgar reigned as toparch of Edessa. To him the Lord Jesus sent . . . a most precious cloth with which He wiped the sweat from His face, and on which shone the Savior's features miraculously reproduced. This displayed to those who gazed on it the likeness and proportions of the body of the Lord.

In the light of the changed Mandylion references, it is significant that, about the beginning of the Eleventh Century, a dramatic alteration in representation of Jesus' burial occurred among those who were painting religious scenes. After that time, pictures were being made depicting the use of a double-length piece of linen, obviously intended to envelop the body as a shroud. On all of these paintings the right hand was crossed over the left at the wrists as the negative image appears on the Shroud of Turin. Several other indications that the Shroud was in Constantinople at this time have been recorded. Included among them is a statement by a Greek, Nicholas Mesarites, who was keeper of the relic collection in the Pharos Chapel. In 1201, when he had to defend the chapel against a mob during a palace revolution, he gave an impassioned speech warning of the sanctity of the shrine in his charge: "In this chapel Christ rises again, and the *sindon* with the burial linens is the clear proof . . . "

A Frenchman who was in Constantinople in 1204 in the army of the Fourth Crusade, Robert de Clari, wrote about some of the fabulous things he saw:

> . . . there was another of the churches which they called My Lady St. Mary of Blachernae, where was kept the sydoine in which Our Lord had been wrapped, which stood [was held] up straight every Friday so that the figure of Our Lord could be plainly seen there . . .

Unfortunately, one of the complicating factors of the Shroud's chronology is that the Crusaders proceeded to sack Constantinople, tearing down and trampling under foot, among other things, the most venerable objects of Christian worship. It was a horrible thing that Christians should so abuse fellow Christians in this manner, yet in only three days Constantinople, the queen of cities, was wrecked in a manner from which she never fully recovered.

In all this confusion the Mandylion (or Shroud?) disappeared. "And no one, either Greek or French, ever knew what became of this sydoine after the city was taken," Robert de Clari wrote.

4

WILSON'S THEORY
OF THE SHROUD
AFTER CONSTANTINOPLE

I N ADDITION TO IAN WILSON, the several sindonologists and various authors who have conjectured on
the whereabouts of the Shroud for a period of one
hundred fifty years after the Constantinople debacle lean
toward the idea that the Knights Templar were its protec-
tors. The thought is that one or more of the Crusaders,
realizing its religious value, secretly took it home from the
Crusades, showed it to their fellow members of the Knights
Templar, and they all dedicated themselves to its
preservation.

Wilson noted that some eighty years before the capture
of Constantinople, the Knights Templar had been founded
by two French knights, Hugh of Payens, Geoffrey of Saint-
Omer and seven of their companions. They called it the
Crusader Order of Knights Templar or "Poor Knights of
Christ of the Temple of Solomon," because they were given
land near the site of the ruined Temple in Jerusalem.

By 1203, they had become wealthy and powerful and had
attracted to their ranks men of the noblest blood, who distinguished themselves as fearless crusaders and who built
across Europe and the Near East a series of virtually
impregnable fortresses. These impenetrable strongholds
were quite important because they were useful as store-

houses for national treasures and valuables of all kinds. Kings and popes alike began to bank with the Templars, giving them the reputation of possessing enormous wealth. The Order of Knights Templar helped finance the Fourth Crusade. When these Crusaders returned, it began to be reported that they were hiding and worshipping a mysterious idol or picture. According to one account, ". . . it was a certain bearded head, which they adored, kissed and called their Savior . . . " Another description was of, "the head of a man with a long reddish beard."

Interestingly enough, a picture probably portraying the "head" the Templars worshipped came to light in England during a severe gale in Somerset in 1951. The ceiling plaster collapsed in an outer building of a cottage belonging to Mrs. A. Topp in the village of Templecombe. Revealed in the roof, covered with coal dust, was a curious panel, the presence of a keyhole and hinge marks, indicating that at one time it had been used as a door. On this panel was a painting of a head, done in distinctly medieval style. It is known that in 1185 the Templars had acquired property in Templecombe and built there a preceptory used for recruiting and training new members of the Order before sending them off for active service in the East. It is also known that the Templars of that time cultivated their beards in the style of the face on the Shroud of Turin. The picture found on the panel in Templecombe is described as having been of a male head with a reddish beard, lifesize, disembodied, and lacking any identification marks. But it was similar in appearance to the icons and paintings from the days of the Mandylion in Constantinople—and thus had the uncanny appearance of being a copy of the Shroud head.

As the Templars continued worshipping their "Savior," in their indomitable way, it became their downfall — because Phillip the Fair, King of France, who had a long cherished plan to confiscate their now legendary wealth, used it as an excuse to accuse them of corruption and "worshipping false idols." Philip's men made a surprise swoop on the Templars' Paris Temple, meeting fierce resistance, conquering and seizing all their goods, but finding no "idol." In England, where similar raids were made and much goods seized, nothing incriminating was found either. Finally, the king killed most of the knights for heresy, torturing many to death. The last two who were recorded being killed as "relapsed heretics" were the Grand Master, Jacques de Molay, and Geoffrey de Charnay. They died declaring that instead of the scandalous sins and iniquities of which they had been accused, the Order of Knights Templar was pure and holy, and had nobly served the cause of Christianity.

The idea here is, then, that the Knights Templar, specifically among the Crusaders, brought the Shroud to France from Constantinople. Since Geoffrey de Charnay was a Templar, it is not surprising then that it came into his possession and eventually into that of his family.

The Known History Of The Shroud Since 1357

However it reached him, we know that Geoffrey de Charny (note spelling), who lived in the Fourteenth Century, was the Shroud's first authenticated owner. Is it possible that Geoffrey de Charnay was his forbear? There is little definite information to connect them. However, it is a relatively rare name, and the difference in spelling would not necessarily be significant because there was seldom standardization in medieval French. In the mid-Fourteenth Century, de Charny, a man of unquestionable integrity, who had been one of France's bravest and most brilliant military leaders, received from King John the Good a "rent" to found a church at Lirey. There was still no mention of the *sindon* during his lifetime, but evidence for his possession of it exists in a medallion preserved in the Musee de Cluny, Paris (Plate No. 7). This is the first known representation of the Shroud entirely full length—with both frontal and dorsal images visible. Two clerics are apparently holding it up over a quaint representation of the Holy Sepulcher, on each side of which are shields bearing coats of arms. The escutcheon on the left side is undoubtedly that of Geoffrey de Charny, as it bears three small silver shields on a red ground. On the right side are the heraldic arms of Jeanne de Vergy, Geoffrey's second wife and subsequent widow.

This surmise postulates that Geoffrey de Charny had inherited the Shroud from the Templars, but was careful not to acknowledge it publicly. His reticence in such circumstances would certainly be understandable because the memory of the recent violent treatment of a possible ancestor was still warm.

7. A pilgrim's medallion depicting the Shroud.

Geoffrey de Charny is reported to have died in 1356 in the Battle of Poitiers, protecting King John, who was fighting Edward, the Black Prince of England. Jeanne de Vergy and their son, Geoffrey II, began to show the *sindon* in the Lirey chapel. Although neither of them ever referred to it as the true Shroud of Jesus, such a rumor circulated freely in the community.

Dozens of "shrouds" were allegedly being shown at this time. Some had images, some did not, but all were put forward as genuine. In the Fourteenth Century, especially, false relics such as "pieces of the true cross" and the "bones of saints," or even "vials of a saint's blood," could be found almost anywhere. Thus, it is not surprising that a few members of the clergy took up the question of the Shroud's authenticity. Particularly vehement was Peter D'Arcis, Bishop of Troyes, in whose diocese the church of Our Lady of Lirey lay. He cited the charge by his predecessor that "after diligent inquiry and examination" he had determined that the cloth was "cunningly painted, the truth being attested by the artist who had painted it." D'Arcis is said to have asked the Pope to issue orders to the Canon at Lirey to cease showing the Shroud as genuine.

The Canon, however, stated that he had permission from a cardinal to display the Shroud, and so he refused to obey the orders of his bishop who wrote to him about it.

Now, a letter from the bishop must have been written, because there are nearly fifty documents that have eventually come to hinge on it. They are letters and instructions to a bailiff to seize the Shroud. This, incidentally, did not take place because the Canon succeeded in hiding it. Also there are edicts from the King regarding this issue, and, a letter from Clement's successor telling the Canon that he was not to present the Shroud with flaming torches and guards of honor, as a genuine article, but only as a symbol for which it stood. And, finally, ironically, the bishop, Peter D'Arcis, was enjoined to refrain from further comment in the future under fear of excommunication.

Jeanne de Vergy remarried, becoming the wife of Aymon of Geneva, a wealthy and influential nobleman who was the uncle of Clement VII. Her son's daughter, Margeruite de Charny, a religious and strong-willed woman, continually refused to turn the *sindon* over to church authorities although frequently ordered to do so, and eventually she suffered excommunication for her unbending position. Her second marriage was to Humbert of Villersexel, a wealthy nobleman, and they took the Shroud eventually to Humbert's domain at St. Hippolyte sur Doubs and stored it in the Chapel des Buessarts, which to this day preserves souvenirs of its stay.

There expositions were held each year and a minicult of the *sindon* appears to have grown up, with many copies of it being made. This conjecture reasons that as Margeruite had no heirs to inherit the cloth, she was intent on finding a place where it would remain in safekeeping.

The Shroud Comes To The House of Savoy

Possibly motivated by the pious reputation of the Savoy family, from which arose the kings of Italy, she eventually decided it should go to Louis I, Duke of Savoy. He was the ruler of a rising dynasty, wealthy and powerful enough to provide the Shroud with adequate security during that troubled period, and also politically influential enough to make the highest dignitaries aware of it. It is not known whether Margeruite gave or sold the Shroud to the House of Savoy, although some reports have it that at least two castles were part of the deal.

For the House of Savoy, the Shroud swiftly became the talisman upon which they depended, and its divine protec-

tion was invoked in difficult times as the family carried it about with them like a holy charm. Thus it was that the Shroud's reputation grew. At that time the famous theologian Francesco della Rovere wrote that the cloth in which the body of Christ was wrapped when He was taken down from the cross "is now preserved with great devotion by the Dukes of Savoy, and it is colored with the blood of Christ."

Within half a century the *sindon* had achieved so much respectability that in 1511 a pilgrimage was made by the future King Francis of France, who was accompanied by Queen Anne of Brittany. It was now recognized publicly as the true Holy Shroud of Jesus.

A ducal church was built at Chambery, the capital of Savoy, to house the Shroud. At its completion an elaborate procession of the Chambery clergy and enormous crowds accompanied the Shroud to its new home. Plate No. 8 is a picture of the Savoy church at Chambery.

Four years later, Pope Julius II approved a chapel as part of the palace complex to be called the Sainte Chapelle of the Holy Shroud, a title giving it the status of a shrine. Unfortunately, on December 4, 1532, there was a fire in the Sainte Chapelle sacristy which caused the extensive burn

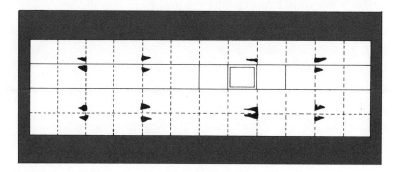

9. The way the cloth was folded prior to the fire. The dark areas show the scorch marks near corners and edges of the folds.

8. The Savoy's Palace at Chambery (facing page).

marks that disfigure the cloth to this day. Plate No. 9 shows the way the cloth was folded prior to the fire, which resulted in the pattern of burns that is still so evident. It was first folded lengthwise twice and then made into a small square exactly one forty-eighth of its entire size.

Public knowledge of the fire motivated many people to suggest that the Shroud had been completely destroyed; but two years later, when the Poor Clare nuns had completed their repair work, and the now blemished *sindon* was once again revealed in public, the rumors were quelled.

The Shroud's owners wanted anew to change its location for its protection. They found a good excuse when Charles Borromeo, the saintly, aged and failing Archbishop of Milan, made it known that he intended to make a pilgrimage on foot to pray in front of it on behalf of the Italian people who were suffering from the plague.

The Duke of Savoy volunteered instead to have the Shroud brought to Turin to save the pilgrim an arduous mountainous journey. Soon after its arrival in Turin in 1578, the chapel where it now resides was especially built for it. The *sindon* was at first displayed annually, but then in order that frequent handling should not damage it needlessly, it was shown only at great events and special occasions, such as royal weddings. In the Nineteenth Century, there were only five expositions, and even less in the Twentieth.

5

OTHER THEORIES OF THE SHROUD'S HISTORY

VERY LITTLE HARD EVIDENCE is available regarding the history of the Shroud, and over the centuries since it was first reported in Lirey in the Fourteenth Century, many different interpretations have been based upon the few reports and hearsay accounts that were available.

What has just been recounted is a feasible interpretation of the early history of the Shroud. It is an interpretation of a handful of historic facts and legends woven into a possible version of what happened. Yet it is so logical that the leaders of the Shroud of Turin Research Project brought Ian Wilson to their New London Symposium to present these hypotheses. Wilson was impressive with his honesty and his knowledge; but he emphatically stated that his opinions were conjectures and should not be considered as facts.

What follows in this chapter is this author's interpretation of the history of the Shroud, based, again, on what little circumstantial and hearsay evidence is available, and on some newly-rediscovered evidence which was apparently not available to Wilson. In addition, some of the theories upon which he bases his tentative conclusions can be interpreted differently. The period during which the Shroud left the Jerusalem area could be much later than Wilson thinks, for example.

The Shroud And The Mandylion

Although it was stated earlier that it was possible that Nicephorus' account of St. Helena's seeing the Shroud was legend, there is just as good a probability that it has some basis in fact. Nicephorus, an ecclesiastical historian, lived in the Thirteenth Century, and when he wrote that St. Helena had seen the Shroud, he was passing along a story that had been in existence for more than nine hundred years.

St. Helena, the mother of Constantine the Great, was a rather remarkable person in her own right. Born in Bithynia in Asia Minor of humble parents, she was about sixty-three when her son became Emperor in 312 A.D., and she converted to Christianity shortly thereafter. At the age of eighty, she went to Jerusalem and became famous for allegedly finding the true cross. Her last days were spent in Palestine, where she built two basilicas, spent much money on church ornamentation, and did other good works for which she was later beatified.

In the year 631, St. Braulion, the Bishop of Saragossa, and a learned and prudent man, wrote, in a letter that has been preserved, of "something that had been well known for a long time—the winding sheet in which the body of the Lord was wrapped." He added, "The scriptures do not tell us that it was preserved, but one cannot call those superstitious who believe in the authenticity of this winding sheet."

Arculph, or Arculphus, who was also mentioned earlier, was a French bishop who travelled to Jerusalem around the year 640. While returning from his pilgrimage to the Holy Land, Arculph was shipwrecked on the shores of Scotland, and having made his way to the religious community on the Island of Iona, he dictated there an account of what he had seen and heard. He stated firmly that he was present in Jerusalem when a shroud was taken from a shrine and shown to a multitude of people. He had even been allowed to kiss it. He said that it was a long piece of linen which gave the impression of being about eight feet in length. "This," says Pierre Barbet, in *A Doctor At Calvary*, "was no small cloth; it was the Shroud."

The above stories, of course, place the idea of the Shroud being taken to King Abgar of Edessa to heal him in a questionable light. What should make this archon of a small city state in what is now known as Turkey so important that the early leaders of Christianity would give up their most sacred relic at his request? There isn't even evidence that Abgar was healed.

In recent years, there have been several unsuccessful attempts to induce healing by exposure to the Shroud. Millions have filed past it during its various displays, but there have been no accounts of miraculous cures. Group Captain G. L. Cheshire, V.C. in *Pilgrimage To The Shroud*, recounts a visit to Turin in 1955 by a crippled Scottish child named Josie Woolam. She was kindly received and permitted to hold the rolled up cloth in her lap. But sadly, her high hopes did not materialize as no cure was reported.

With the destruction of Jerusalem by Titus in 70 A.D., most Jewish people dispersed throughout the world and many became the bankers of those times. How intriguing it would be if one could prove that Christian Jews hid and saved this cloth from destruction. Could it have been taken to Edessa by them? A possible conjecture as to the date of the movement of the *sindon* from Jerusalem to Edessa could be about 700 A.D., when turmoil throughout Christianity arose concerning the question of images. This was similar to the much later period of the Reformation, when Protestants attacked relics as works of the devil. If, for example, there had been a monastery on the Jordan that had been showing the Shroud of Jesus, the iconoclasts, as those opposed to religious relics were termed, could have been pretty hostile to them. This would seem a likely time for those monks—who might be called the Brothers of the

Cloth—to move their precious object to Edessa for safe keeping. Yet even there persecutions were not behind them, and once again believers were forced to hide the *sindon*. Is that when it was folded in four so that just the head showed, and it became known as the Mandylion? We have to wonder how long the Mandylion was hidden in Edessa. All accounts indicate that after its removal to Constantinople it was given into the custody of the Eastern Church; and, after it was discovered that it was a *sindon* and not just a portrait, it was displayed at full length as Wilson has reported. This is confirmed by writings of some who viewed it.

How The Shroud Moved To France

One of the principal questionable areas of this conjectured history is how the Shroud was moved from the dying city of Constantinople to France. And in this writer's opinion, nothing is more doubtful than the idea that it was turned over to members of the militant order of Knights Templar. They had previously been favored by kings and popes, but the political and religious climate had changed by 1204. Suspicion of them was rife all over Europe, and investigations began in the early 1300s in France, England, Germany, Spain and Portugal. In 1309, Clement V abolished the order, and in 1314 its leaders were tortured and then executed by Philip IV of France. This Philip, called "The Fair," was the great enemy of the Templars, and he eventually confiscated most of the Order's wealth, giving its lands to the Knights of St. John, who became the Knights of Malta. Certainly at this time if any Templars had been asked to provide security for the passage of the Shroud out of Constantinople, the last place they would have taken it would have been the domain of their principal enemy.

At that time, the ecclesiastical power in Rome was actively striving to increase its influence and become heir in fact to the secular authority of the Holy Roman Empire. The eastern branch of the empire was in the process of being subjugated by the Turks. There was no love lost between Rome and Constantinople, but leaders of the latter must have had to overcome their distrust and distaste in order to plead for military assistance from the Eternal City. They probably offered great religious and art treasures as recompense. Both the emperors of the East and the West would have wanted to be as sure as possible that the Shroud would reach Rome, and it hardly seems likely that they would have turned over the most precious relic in all Christendom to the Knights Templar.

The following conjectures questioning involvement by the Knights Templar, which are based on historical evidence, are strengthened by the catalogue, dated 1247, for the Empire's religious possessions. This inventory, referred to in the monumental work in Italian by Mons. Pietro Savio (*Richerche Storiche Sulla Sindone*, 1957), lists the Shroud as part of these possessions. The fact that this revered relic was reported to be still in Constantinople in the middle of the Thirteenth Century, together with other details of this Order's history, would appear to sound the death knell of this popular theory.

Also, why should the references to the Templars worshipping a "head" pertain to the burial cloth? Why would it have been just a head at a time when the entire *sindon* was now known to exist? Perhaps they'd had a portrait painted after seeing the Shroud displayed on Fridays at the Church of St. Mary of Balachernae in Constantinople. The question of the head having a red beard could further point to a portrait separate from the *sindon*. There is no logical reason why these Christian Knights should not have revered a likeness as others did their icons and crucifixes; it did not have to be the real thing. There is no evidence to support the charge of their worshipping idols when the greed and the struggle for power by the French king and his followers resulted in the Templars' property being seized and its leaders executed. There was no such object found.

If the Templars did not transport the Shroud to France, then who did? Judging by what is noted in the little bit of evidence and the miniscule written records available, whoever carried it would have had to be on a covert mission. When the Romans came at the behest of the Eastern Emperor, despite the intent of the leaders, the soldiers proceeded to loot the city, and so the Shroud must have been secreted away for safety's sake.

The fact that the cloth wound up in France would indicate that perhaps French knights had been chosen by the Emperor of the East to carry it. And it would have been a hazardous journey even with a company of soldiers, for they had to travel through the lines of the Turks and the Serbs into what is now Yugoslavia and thence to Rome. But why, then, did the Shroud not reach its intended destination?

The plague was common in those times. The black death could have overtaken all but one of the emissaries. The survivor, weakened and possibly even ill himself, could have struggled to his home to die, with the Shroud hidden under his saddle. But as he was a vassal of the French king, the sacred secret this knight carried with him would undoubtedly have become known to his ruler.

At this time Philip VI reigned in France. He had ambitions to be recognized as the Holy Roman Emperor, so his desires clashed with those of the Pope. His church advisors would point out that his owning the Shroud would present a very ticklish situation. He had already challenged the Church's temporal power by appointing his own supporters to be the nobility of the church—the bishops and the abbots. He had even chosen his own father-confessor, thereby eliminating the Pope's best intelligence source in his court. Coming out into the open as possessor of Christ's winding sheet would have intensified an already weak position; he would have been asking for excommunication. So, he probably made certain that this revered relic was turned over for safe keeping to a trusted abbot. The Pope and his advisors would thus realize that King Philip was extending his protection to it, but they would be unable to do anything about the situation.

Other historians project other ideas about the possible journey of the Shroud from Constantinople at the time of the Crusades. A theory put forth by the Rev. Father Solaro in his *La S. Sindone* is quoted by Vignon, who admits that it is but a supposition, but feels it to be important nonetheless.

Vignon says, in *The Shroud Of Christ*, that Father Solaro mentioned that when the crusaders sacked the city of Constantinople, they respected the shrine of St. Mary of Blachernae. This is an historic fact testified to by Count Riant in his *Exuviae*, Vignon says. The count stated that Garnier de Trainel, Bishop of Troyes, who accompanied the expedition, was given the duty of preserving all the relics which had been found in the Imperial Chapel, having full power over them all, to deal with as seemed best to him. This bishop sent considerable numbers of valuables and relics to Europe. And while the list of them is known, there is no mention of the Holy Shroud. Father Solaro reasoned that the precious relic was preserved by the bishop for himself. This may have been done to improve security during the homeward journey. As it happened, however, the bishop never returned—he died at Constantinople in the year 1205.

What, then, became of the Holy Shroud? The names of most of the bishop's subordinates are known, and Father Solaro supposes that it passed into one of their hands. They were chiefly natives of Champagne; one of them at least was related to the Count de Charnay, he says. The Shroud might thus have passed surreptitiously into the possession of the de Charnay family. "But," says Vignon, ". . . we must once more admit that this is probability and not proof."

There is no historical fact on which can be based an explanation of how the Shroud came into the possession of Geoffrey I, Le Compte de Charny and Lord of Champagne. We do know that in 1353 he turned over the *sindon* to the Abbey of Lirey. There is a legend that he had received it as a reward of valor. It is a fact that in 1355, as one of France's greatest knights, he was appointed Grand Standard Bearer by King John, who had succeeded Philip. He died beside his king in the battle against the English led by the Black Prince at Poitiers on September 19, 1356.

Before his death, the de Charny family had again taken protective custody of the Shroud. There was warfare and pestilence in Champagne, and this noble family had the resources to protect it, which the Abbot of Lirey did not. However, later an ecclesiastical court in 1418 again ordered Geoffrey's granddaughter, Marguerite, to turn over the *sindon* to the church at Lirey. The long arm of the Church was no doubt trying to acquire what was felt to be its property. She insisted the initial transfer had only been a loan, and she refused several orders to relinquish it, until eventually she was excommunicated. After her husband died a few years later, the cloth became the focal point of Marguerite's life. Everywhere she went, it went with her. She did not part with it until 1453, thirty-five years after the court had ruled against her.

The Shroud Comes To The House Of Savoy

In some way, she had to capitulate since it came into the hands of Louis I of Savoy under circumstances that have been described as "somewhat murky." One report is that Marguerite de Charny received two castles named Mirabel and Flumet from the duke. By contrast, another account says that this aging woman was deeply concerned to have the ban of excommunication lifted. And it was: she was again able to participate in mass before she died. There must be some reason why the Church lifted its edict—most probably because she had complied with several orders of the ecclesiastical court to return the Shroud to Lirey. It may be assumed that Marguerite did give back her precious relic to the authorities and received absolution. Then the church hired agents to carry the cloth to Rome.

They probably would have sent dummy packages with other representatives, particularly if they had any indication that word of the intended mission had leaked out. Their efforts were to no avail. In Italy, henchmen of the Duke of Savoy intercepted the church's emissaries and took possession of the *sindon*. This scenario of events would embrace both the apparently contradictory facts of Savoy acquiring possession and the church lifting its ban, and would include the duke "acquiring" it from the church.

Such action would have been in keeping with the times. Savoy had to be strong and ruthless to have laid the foundation he did for his family. What he wanted, he took. And, certainly, at that period, his power was such that even the Pope could not challenge him; his possessions were too large and the church's income therefrom was too great. If this possible explanation is correct, it is interesting to reflect on the fact that the Savoy family grew in power over the centuries until it controlled all of Italy.

The 1898 exposition at which the cloth was first photographed was held to celebrate the Sardinian Constitution on which the nation was based. The Vatican had by then become a small state within the City of Rome. The ambition of the church hierarchy to be another Holy Roman Empire had vanished, but one could say the Shroud had finally reached its destination. Umberto II, the deposed king in exile, still has legal title to the *sindon*, but the Mother Church controls it through Archbishop Ballestrero of Turin.

There is another intriguing version of why Marguerite transferred her prized possession to Louis I of Savoy at his residence in Chambery. In his book, *File On The Shroud*, David Sox recounts the legend that she

> gave the cloth to Duke Louis because when she was returning to Burgundy her relic-bearing mule stopped at the gate of Chambery and refused to budge.

However, as Sox commented further, "that explanation is as apocryphal as it is charming."

In conclusion, this author believes his conjectures on the movement of the Shroud from Constantinople to Lirey, and thence to Chambery are more in accord with the historical and religious background of the period. However, it is important to remember that this version of its history prior to the mid-Fifteenth Century and Ian Wilson's theory are both feasible interpretations of the sketchy records and legends of the past that are available. As new information is unearthed, other explanations may become feasible as well.

What is known for certain is its possession by the de Charny; that somehow it became the property of the Dukes of Savoy; that it was recognized and venerated as an authentic religious relic in their church at Chambery; and that it was finally moved to Turin in 1578. No truly scientific research into its authenicity was performed until a revealing photograph was taken in 1898.

6

PHOTOGRAPHY
REVEALS A MYSTERY

THE YEAR 1898 was an important one in the history of the Shroud. It was the fiftieth anniversary of the formation of the Kingdom of Italy, and in Turin a three-part exhibition was planned, based on industrial exhibits, art shows and a religious presentation.

Secondo Pia, from the nearby city of Asti, was chosen to head the art exhibit. This lawyer had been a councilman and the mayor of his home city. He was thoroughly imbued with the idea that the works of artists from the northwest of Italy were just as great as those of Florence, Rome or Naples; and he had spent twenty-five years in dedicated efforts to prove his point. To do this, he had learned photography, a relatively new technique about which not a great deal was yet known. Those who were partially skilled guarded their knowledge carefully. Helping anybody else understand it would only provide a competitor, they thought, and proficiency was the basis for a lucrative profession.

Pia had, by trial and error, laboriously made himself into a first-class photographer. He had had a great deal of experience working with reflectors in dark, gloomy old churches, but he knew nothing about taking pictures in buildings lit by the newly-invented electric lights, so he spent months in an effort to learn proper procedures.

No one knows whether Secondo Pia was the individual who suggested to King Umberto I that the Shroud be photographed at the time of this religious exposition. Whoever it was found the King very reluctant, for he was honestly puzzled by the problem of how to handle reproductions of the Shroud. Would these pictures, he wondered, have to receive the same degree of reverence as the Holy Cloth itself? He was only persuaded that a photographic record would be worthwhile when someone pointed out to him that if there were a major catastrophe such as a volcanic eruption, *then* black marble might not be protection enough for the genuine Shroud and photographic copies would be invaluable.

It was planned that Secondo Pia would be allowed a few hours on the opening day in May in order to photograph the *sindon* after it was hung in the main sanctuary. To make this possible, he had to construct a platform which could be bolted together quickly and on which he could erect his Voigtlander camera, his lights and his reflectors.

On the 25th of May, a very solemn high mass was celebrated in the Royal Chapel. Present were three archbishops, many other church dignitaries, the Duke of Aosta, and other members of the royal family. These included the Princess Clothilde, who in 1868 had put a new red silk backing on the Shroud, doing the entire work on her knees, using tiny, beautiful stitches as she performed her labor of love.

Following the mass, the Duke of Aosta handed over the small red velvet bag containing the keys, and the senior archbishop approached the grille above the altar. Behind this were three locks into which he inserted the three keys and turned them. This opened up the chest out of which two young priests hauled a long wooden box. Within this wooden box was the beautiful four-foot-long silver container which is the repository of the Holy Shroud.

Priests had placed a long table conveniently near the altar, and on this the cloth was reverently unwrapped, inch by inch. Those present were permitted to kiss it, then it was carefully re-rolled and taken out to the main sanctuary where, after it was affixed to a board backing, it was placed in a gilded frame hung high above the altar (Plate No. 12).

There had been a moment of consternation, for the previously prepared wooden backing on which it was to be mounted was revealed to be shorter than the *sindon*. After a quick decision by the senior archbishop, one end of the cloth was folded under before it was placed in the frame. Consequently, the 1898 pictures taken by Pia are readily identifiable because the feet are missing.

Thousands of people passed to see it, and mass was celebrated almost continuously. After the installation, the church was cleared, and Pia hurried to erect his scaffold and to set up his camera. While he was using a long time exposure, the diffusing glass of his Voightlander camera broke with a crackling sound, caused by the heat of the lights and reflectors. Since his first effort had failed, it was necessary to make another attempt three days later, and this was successful. He obtained two time exposures on glass plates. Then he took a hansom cab back to his apartment. He put a plate into a tank of developing fluid, watched anxiously, and then saw an image begin to form on the glass.

When he picked it up, he almost dropped it in amazement! For what he was looking at was not the usually confusing photographic negative, but a clear positive image. The lights and shadows were reversed from those on the cloth and, oddly enough, they were far more lifelike and realistic, showing details never before observed on the Shroud.

In order to understand the incredible mystery that came to light at this moment in time, it is necessary to remember the basics of photography. During the latter half of the

10. Positive and negative photographs of Pope Pius XI.

Twentieth Century, most people are familiar with what a negative looks like. But Plate No. 10 brings out the fundamental facts that have to be considered before one can grasp the problem with which one is faced. It will also help to evaluate and determine the validity of the hypothesis being outlined.

This picture of Pope Pius XI shows him in a printed form on the left side. On the right, is the negative of this print. One quickly remembers how unusual negatives are, how different they are from the finished prints. In the positive on the left, one sees how the Pope's face, cassock with its ermine trim, skull cap and hand are all shades of white. In the negative, though, they appear as varying densities of black. The color tones are all reversed. This reversal of tonality can be seen also in the shading of the eyes and under the chin. In analyzing the negative and the positive prints of the Shroud of Turin, this is what one has to remember: in a negative image all color and shading is reversed.

In other words, in any negative there should be only a rearrangement of lights and shadows and a reversal of position. Light areas should become dark and dark areas should become light. The left should be right, and the right, left. Pia's result, then, should have been the usual abnormal

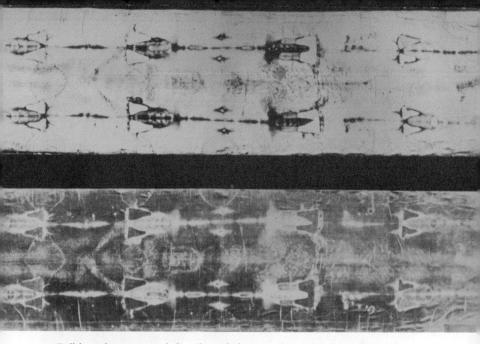

11. Full length pictures of the Shroud showing frontal (left) and dorsal (right) images of the body.

caricature of the original that would be understandable only when it was printed in the positive. Instead, his negative was a positive portrait.

Now consider a picture of the Shroud as the eye sees it (Plate No. 11). This is the way one would have observed it had one been in the cathedral at that time. On the left one sees the frontal image of the man on the Shroud. On the right is a dorsal image. The lines below the top quarter and up one quarter from the bottom are from the fire in 1532. One can see the dark scorched places and the white patches where the Poor Clares replaced the burned-out portions. One can also see the stains from the water that was used to put out the fire in the Sacristy of Sainte Chappelle in Chambery in that year. The lozenge-shaped stains are particularly noticeable in the center of the front image, along the bottom of the cloth, and between the front and back images of the head.

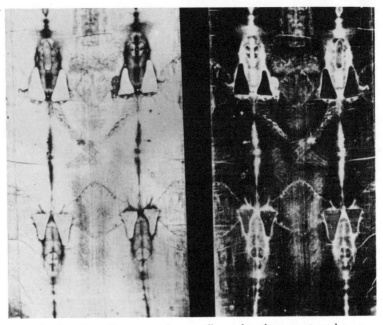

12. Left, the Shroud as viewed normally; right, the negative plate as Pia saw it in 1898.

One can imagine the shock of the sight that greeted Secondo Pia's eyes when he pulled that plate from the developing tank on the 28th day of May, 1898. In this picture (Plate No. 12, right) one can see only the front half. The cloth, instead of having that ivory tone seen to the left is now black: it is a negative; it is reversed. The brown stains, the scorched areas down both sides, are no longer a burnt brown color, they are white; they are a negative. The white patches that filled the holes from that terrible fire are not white any more, they're black; they're a negative. But those tannish, vague, diffused stains that one sees with the naked eye on the cloth are no longer that way. There is a clear, positive image. It is no wonder that Secondo Pia nearly dropped the plate.

Plate No. 11 shows the Shroud stretched out to its full length, the top picture revealing it as the eye views it. Below is the negative of the same view. Here one can see the contrast especially clearly.

Plate No. 12 shows just the frontal view, both as the eye sees it and as a negative. The face on the left is vague and diffused as compared to the face on the right. Narrowing the subject down, Plate No. 13 shows the heads, side by side. The half-circle at the top is a water stain. The lines running across are creases in the thin cloth. It is well to look at this carefully in view of the evidence that has developed recently from scientific analysis. The white area on either side of the face between the head and the hair in the negative imprint and the black area in a like position on the positive face should be noticed. Many scientists are of the opinion that this is the image of the cloth that held up the jaws-in-death, as was customary in a traditional Jewish burial of the period.

However, recently some scientists, using image enhancement techniques, have discovered what they believe

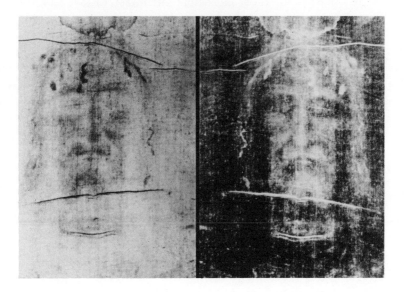

13. Negative and Positive images of the face on the Shroud.

is body image in this area. These researchers have stated that the fainter image area is due to a variation in the weave of the cloth, as is common in hand-processed flax. The realization that the Shroud contained a negative image was shocking not only to Secondo Pia but to His Majesty, King Umberto I and all his principal advisors. A stream of highly placed people journeyed to Secondo Pia's apartment to view this astonishing development. Generally, it was felt that, after informing the Vatican, the situation should be carefully considered before a public announcement was made. Efforts to keep it quiet failed, for eventually one of the court, who was a newspaper publisher, could contain the secret no longer, and he released the story.

People at that time knew little or nothing about photographic principles. Those who did know had kept it to themselves. Editors, as well, fell into this classification. Consequently, the most incredible mishmash of fact and fancy showed up in all the leading newspapers of the world, because the editors did not understand the basic principles involved.

One individual who saw these reports was Catholic historian Abbe Ulysse Chevalier, a medieval specialist who had compiled a very valuable index of documents from the Middle Ages. He remembered and dug up the information that was to darken Pia's name for many years—a document that is extraordinary because it is a monumental example of hearsay evidence. As discussed above, it purported to be the draft of a letter from Bishop Peter D'Arcis that sustained his argument that the Shroud was only a painting, based on a predecessor's verbal statement.

Ulysse Chevalier put this into a monograph along with the forty-nine documents hinging on it referred to earlier, attacking the authenticity of the Shroud, his conclusion based upon this questionable, so-called evidence from the bishop in the Fourteenth Century. But it was enough to close the discussion, and the president of the *Academie des Inscriptions*, at a solemn sitting held on November 15, 1901, while awarding a gold medal of 1,000 francs to M. Chevalier,

> did not hesitate to severely censure any future attempt to impose upon the credulity of the faithful with what could henceforth be described only as a fraudulent misrepresentation.

Father Herbert Thurston of the Society of Jesus, one of the era's greatest intellects, picked up this monograph in London and supported it. He wrote a condemnatory article on the Shroud of Turin for the *Catholic Encyclopaedia*, 1910 edition. It was not until 1957 that this point of view was refuted by Rev. Walter Abbott, S.J., in an article in a supplemental volume of this encyclopaedia. A more current analysis was presented in 1963 by Father Adam Otterbein, C.ss.R.,President of the Holy Shroud Guild.

The English-speaking peoples are primarily Protestant; and one of the fundamental facts of the Reformation was the rejection of the use of relics. The resultant effect has been far reaching, so much so that until very recently when there has been a good bit of media publicity, very little has been known about the Shroud among English-speaking peoples. The Order of Redemptorists, of course, propagates knowledge of this cloth in the United States; but their efforts are mainly acceptable to those of the Catholic faith. American Protestants have been conditioned to spurn, almost as an act of faith, such souvenirs from the past. An identical reaction appears to have manifested in Great Britain, Australia, New Zealand and South Africa. So Ulysse Chevalier and Fr. Thurston between them caused most people, figuratively, to wash their hands of the Shroud of Turin for many years.

Secondo Pia had to wait thirty-three years to be vindicated. Very little was said or done scientifically about the Shroud until it was shown again in May, 1931, during a twenty-one-day exposition when two million people viewed it. By this time, cameras had improved immeasurably. The tradition of hiding one's knowledge of photography to discourage competition had been discarded with World War I, when the camera became valuable as a military tool. There were now diopter lenses—lenses that magnified as they photographed. Such developments vastly improved techniques and materials at all stages of the photographic process. Schools had been established during the war to teach men to use cameras, and the new science of photography was now out in the open, with competition resulting in increasingly better instruments. So in 1931 there were many good photographers available.

Once again, a man from Turin was asked to be the official photographer. He was Giuseppe Enrie, the editor of *Vita Photographica Italiana* and owner of a studio and laboratory in that city. On at least one occasion the Shroud was taken down from its perch and placed at the foot of the altar where he could view it better. Once, even, it was revealed to him without its glass covering. He took a number of photographs of the *sindon*, and, to avoid the same kind of charges of fraud that had plagued Secondo Pia after his 1898 photographs had been distributed around the world, Enrie invited five professional photographers to study his plates. They verified that none of them had been retouched and that all had accurately captured what the naked eye could see on the surface of the Shroud. They signed a document that swore to these conclusions.

From then on, Pia's photographs were retired, and the Enrie photographs became the official pictures of the Shroud that were given out by ecclesiastical authorities in Turin. Appropriately, Secondo Pia acted as one of Enrie's assistants, while Paul Vignon was another. The evil gossip that Secondo Pia had faked the original by retouching the negative was proved to be false. Secondo Pia's good name had been restored.

Chevalier's condemnatory monograph had results that the sincere, but mistaken, priest and historian could not have anticipated. It challenged the common sense and scientific judgment of an outstanding intellect at a great university in Paris.

7

VIGNON'S RESEARCH

GOING BACK TO THE RESEARCH at the end of the last century, one comes to a professor of comparative anatomy at the Sorbonne in Paris named Yves Delage, who was near the zenith of a career in zoology, physics and mathematics. Delage had been born to Catholic parents, but had turned to agnosticism. He was, nonetheless, open minded enough to be horrified at the attitude taken by Chevalier and the others who accepted theories of forgery without testing them.

Delage said, in effect, this is ridiculous and unscientific for people approaching the Twentieth Century. In the last one hundred years, we have seen more scientific advancement than in the previous thousands of years. Now, here on a cloth, we have a negative impression that has existed for nearly five hundred years, at least, before the invention of photography. We must investigate it because it would be unscientific to do otherwise. And it would be particularly unscientific to take hearsay evidence from a bishop dead five hundred years and to brush aside an incredible mystery.

But Delage, himself, did not have the time to devote to this challenge.

Fortunately for him, a former student who had recently

received his doctorate of science, Paul Vignon, was available to do the research. Vignon, a young botanist who subsequently became professor of biology at the Institut Catholique in Paris, had many attributes that suited him for the task Delage wished him to carry out. He was also the ideal person to be the pioneer investigator of the Shroud.

In the first place, he was independently wealthy, and did not have to make a living with his work. He had the necessary scientific background to approach the problem, and he was a first-class artist with the visual sense and knowledge of pigments which, combined with his training in chemistry and biology, were valuable assets. Vignon had heard about the image on the Shroud, and had been excited at first. But then he had read Chevalier's monograph and had put the subject out of his mind. Delage reawakened his interest; and Vignon, with the promise that he might use Delage's laboratory on his return, traveled to Turin.

In the Italian city, Vignon talked to Secondo Pia and obtained two copies of his plates. He also discovered that two other pictures had been taken: one by a priest, a snapshot; and the other, a time exposure by a police officer. Neither was of any research value, but both photographs proved the negative quality of the image on the cloth and confirmed Pia's original work.

Taking his copies back with him to Paris, Vignon established himself in Delage's laboratory and went to work. The first thing he did was to tackle the question of painting.

Plate No. 14 shows a picture of a portion of the cloth itself. The material is linen, commonly used in ancient Palestine for gravecloths. Magnified seven times, it shows a three to one weft: that is, a three over one weave of flax in a herringbone pattern.

The Shroud has been the basis for more textile research than was ever dreamed possible, as far as ancient weavings are concerned. As a result, it has been found that there is no

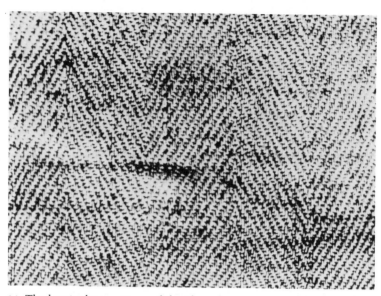

14. The herringbone pattern of the Shroud weave.

problem regarding the age of the cloth; it could be two thousand years old. In fact, similar cloths have been found in the Pyramids, and ancient Egyptians were very proficient in weaving this type of material. Cloth fifteen hundred years older than the age claimed for the Shroud has been found. It is quite possible that the Jews acquired proficiency in this type of weaving during their enslavement in Egypt. The thread appears to be hand-spun, an ancient technique. After about 1200 A.D., European thread was spun with the wheel. Finally, the threads are believed to have been bleached before weaving, which was also an ancient practice.

The thing that struck Vignon so forcibly was that under magnification there is no sign of pigment in the cloth. He experimented, and bear in mind that he was a proficient artist. He researched and discovered every type of paint that had been used by anyone during the Middle Ages. Testing them on cloth, he found that it was impossible to use paint on cloth and not have a residue left between the strands.

Likewise, experiments with dyes ruled them out. Such a liquid solution could not be controlled on cloth; it would seep down into the threads so that blots were frequent. Vignon was forced to the conclusion that the markings on the cloth were not painted or dyed; they are the result of being imprinted in some manner. Further, he attempted to paint a negative, but he found that it was utterly impossible. No man, he maintained, could paint a negative. A good illustration of his point would be that one can't expect a blind man to paint a picture of a face. No one can paint what he can't see. There had to be some other explanation of the image on the cloth of the Shroud of Turin other than paint.

Vignon took his findings to Yves Delage and received the approval of this great scientist. Despite the way people had clung to the suspect statement, based on hearsay, of the Bishop of Troyes from the Fourteenth Century, claiming the Shroud was a fraud, Vignon and Delage both agreed that it had been proved beyond any doubt that the figure on the *sindon* was not painted.

If it was not painted, how was the image formed? In his careful study of the prints furnished by Secondo Pio, Vignon noticed a very significant feature. There seemed to be, throughout, a relationship between the closeness one would expect the cloth to have to certain portions of the body and the varying strength of the image. The eyes, for example, look like bottomless pools on the negative image of the Shroud. The line of the nose is clear but the markings are not as strong in the hollow that is formed between the nose and the cheekbone. The most indicative area, probably, is the left leg. The man on the Shroud had his left leg nailed over the right leg and it is very obvious that rigor mortis had occurred in the left limb. There is a crook in the knee. The markings on the back of the left calf are not nearly as distinct as those on the back of the right calf. This led Vignon to think about projection, and to eventually form his vaporgraphic hypothesis. This was to become an important consideration for future studies.

There had been some interesting work done by Rene Colson, a professor at the Ecole Polytechnique in Paris, who had been experimenting with the effects of zinc vapors at a distance. Dr. Colson had placed carvings coated with zinc in a box, with a photographic plate lying several inches away, and the box was sealed from outside air movement. On the photographic plate he had obtained a negative image of the carvings. Vignon went to Colson and they worked together testing this same technique again. In twenty-four hours, they succeeded in getting a negative image of a head and a medallion.

So far, so good. But what could possibly have projected from the skin of the man on the Shroud, and what could have been on the cloth to react to something from the skin?

Vignon made an intuitive jump. What was the burial fluid of the Jews? Colson read the Old Testament in the Greek and found the pertinent portion, a Mosaic recipe for preparation of an anointing oil which was also used as a funeral ointment. This called for the combination of olive oil, myrrh, and aloes in a loose paste. The last named, aloes, is a plant with very strong medicinal properties, and it breaks down into two major chemical derivatives: aloin and aloetin. The scientist Colson recalled that aloetin oxidized readily in conjunction with alkalies.

A test proved it. They took a strip of linen cloth and moistened it with ammoniacal water, and this they dipped into a mixture of olive oil and aloes. The result was a faint yellowish-tan stain of the same tone as that found on the Shroud of Turin.

But how could ammonia vapors come from a human body?

Another intuitive jump was made which, when checked

with chemists, proved to be correct. An individual who dies in great agony has what is called febrile, or morbid, sweat. This sweat is very heavy in urea, and the fermentation of urea results in the chemical change to carbonate of ammonia. This compound consistently gives off ammoniacal vapors. After many months of detailed experimentation, the basic secret underlying the *sindon* seemed no longer a mystery to the researchers.

The findings of these men showed that if a cloth soaked with this loose paste of olive oil, myrrh and aloes is placed on a dead body that died in agony, and, consequently, with copious quantities of urea in the sweat, a negative image can be formed by the ammoniacal vapors acting on the aloetin. However, and this is the heart of the matter, the image appears only if the cloth stays undisturbed on a body for between twenty-four and thirty-six hours *and* is removed before putrefaction sets in.

There was one snag; Vignon and Colson and all those who have since repeated this experiment, with similar results, have produced a blurred image.

Research has developed two aspects of this problem. In Dr. Vignon's experiment the ammoniacal vapors could never reproduce a clear and distinct image, as on the Shroud. The principle was demonstrated, but the results were not comparable. As members of the Shroud of Turin Research Project pointed out, gas diffuses in all directions. The negative likeness would appear to require vertical projection of gas, energy, radiation or whatever, to produce such a well-defined figure.

In contemporary research, blood stains posed a similar problem. As cloth adhered to them, it was found that there was no way to remove a simulated covering without smearing them. No such effects are found on the original.

This interesting experimentation led to the amazing situation of the agnostic, the brilliant scientist Yves Delage, taking the findings of his young colleague, Paul Vignon, before the most august body of scientific opinion in the world at that time, the French Academy of Sciences. The announcement that he would speak on such a subject caused a sensational stir. The room was more packed on the twenty-first day of April, 1902, than it had been when Pasteur had made the report of his findings regarding the treatment for rabies by inoculation.

Yves Delage told his listeners of the existence of a strip of linen supposed to be the Shroud of Christ. He briefly detailed its history and showed the pictures taken by Secondo Pia. He explained the problem of negativity revealed by these photographs that had given rise to the whole question, and had led him and his colleagues into the fields of chemistry, physics and physiology in their pursuit of the truth about it.

"The question poses itself as to how this image was made," he said. Then he spoke of Vignon's painstaking studies and his conclusion that the stain image could not possibly be a painting, either directly or by inversion of colors. He described the bloodstains, etc., and revealed Vignon's conclusion that the Shroud is not a painting made by a human hand, but that it had been obtained by some physiochemical phenomenon.

Then Delage dared to ask these fellow scientists if he might speak of the identity of the person whose image appears on the *sindon*. He said the Shroud told plainly of a victim who had been crucified, flogged, pierced in the side and crowned with thorns. On the other hand, there was the story of Christ's Passion, which spoke just as plainly of a man who had suffered these very punishments. "Is it not natural to bring these two parallel series together and tie them to the same object?" he asked.

He paused a moment, and then went on:

Let us add to this that, in order for the image to have
formed itself without being ultimately destroyed, it was
necessary that the corpse remain in the shroud at least
twenty-four hours, the amount of time needed for the
formation of the image, and at the most several days,
after which putrification sets in which destroys that
image, and finally the shroud tradition — more or less
aprocryphal, I would say — tells us that this is precisely
what happened to Christ; dead on Friday and —
disappeared — on Sunday.

Then, gravely, Delage made his final affirmation:
"The man of the Shroud is the Christ." This bold statement
caused a tremendous sensation. The membership of the
French Academy was composed mostly of free thinkers,
agnostics, and atheists—many were bitterly anti-church.
They took decided views, pro and con. The secretary, M.
Berthelot, was so upset that he withdrew part of Delage's
findings from the official notes of the meeting. The first
report did not include the whole story, which only added to
the confusion and minimized the effect of the remarkable
research conducted by Vignon.

It was necessary for Delage to turn to magazines and
scientific articles to prove his point, which he did. Then he
made a very interesting observation. In effect, he said, what
men's minds were boggling at was the identity of the man
on the Shroud. They weren't questioning the scientific findings *per se*. If the man on the Shroud had been Sargon or
Achilles or one of the Pharaohs, there would have been no
question. It was the fact that the man on the Shroud was
the Founder of Christianity that was just too much to
accept for the mind of those scientifically inclined.

When the medical approach of Dr. Pierre Barbet was
added to these initial studies, the foundation for all the
scientific research on the Shroud had been laid.

8

BARBET AND HIS
MEDICAL RESEARCH

Another pioneer scientific contributor to our understanding of the Shroud was Dr. Pierre Barbet, chief surgeon at St. Joseph's Hospital in Paris. He clarified the anatomical details by experimentation. Thus, he revealed the exactitude that could be achieved about many of the Shroud's features that had not been clear before that time. Since his hospital provided one of the city's largest teaching facilities, he had at his disposal excellent conditions for experimental work on both corpses and amputated limbs. Following are plates which reveal some of his significant findings.

Plate No. 15 is limited to the positive image of the head in the middle of a negative. It has been said that,

> The more one studies it, the more does it stir the soul. It inspires and it subdues. It appeals and it challenges. It has a message for every heart, if only one will read it aright.

It is a mixture of sovereignty and sorrow. The peace that surpasses understanding and a still strength are in strange contrast to the sadistic savagery with which the body was treated. The late Father Edward A. Wuenschel expressed it in *Self Portrait of Christ*, "It is a face that bears the imprint of a superior spirit unbroken by suffering and unconquered by death."

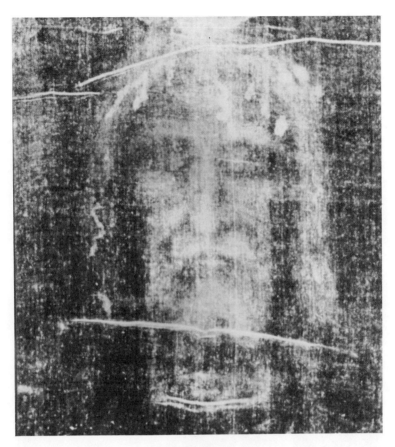

15. The positive image of the Shroud face.

It was from this very negative, among others, however, that Pierre Barbet was able to conjecture about the nature of the depicted wounds. He observed that the face had received a very heavy blow, or blows, on the right cheek, for this area is badly swollen. The swelling encompasses even the eyelid. The doctors of medicine who have carefully studied the enlarged photographs of the Shroud say that the bones of the man on the Shroud were not broken; but the nose is swollen as if the nasal cartilage had been fractured.

One can see that there is blood in the hair. Dr. Barbet identified it as real, clotted blood. One observes that this man on the *sindon* had his scalp lacerated in many places, resulting in a considerable loss of blood. One will notice the flow down the forehead that looks like a figure three. It breaks in the middle as if there were a crease at that point of the skin, which a furrowed brow would cause. At the bottom of the figure three there is a break, and below that a large drop. It has been suggested that this fits exactly what would happen if there had been a band across the brow and around the head. The blood would have flowed down, turned sideways as it reached the furrow in the skin, continued down to another furrow, then hit an obstacle, flowed over it, and created the drop above the left eyebrow.

On the left of the next picture, (Plate No. 16), one sees the portion from the neck to the buttocks of the dorsal image. It is magnified on the right. One notes that this man on the Shroud received a very heavy scourging, or flogging.

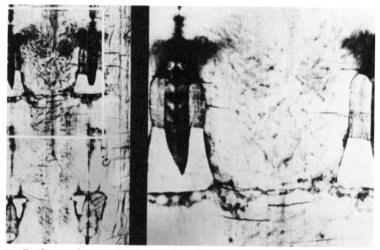

16. Evidence of scourging on the dorsal image.

Plate No. 17 shows two examples of a Roman flagrum; short-handed, postilion-type whips with long strands on the ends of which were little dumbbells made of bone, or ivory, or metal. On the left, one sees the actual magnified markings on the Shroud, representing the markings on the body of the image on the Shroud.

It is difficult to find the right word to describe this kind of punishment. Perhaps scourging is the best one can do. It is not flogging in the sense of laying a whip across an individual; forty blows would kill anybody if the entire stripe were laid across the body, drawing blood. The Jewish law in Deuteronomy states that no man shall receive more than forty blows. The Jews, in fact, were careful to limit the number of blows on a criminal to thirty-nine for fear of breaking this law. The only limitation in Roman law was that a citizen could not be given this punishment. The cloth very plainly shows that it wasn't the laying on of stripes. The executioners were skilled enough in their brutal task to hit just the skin with the ends of the dumbbells.

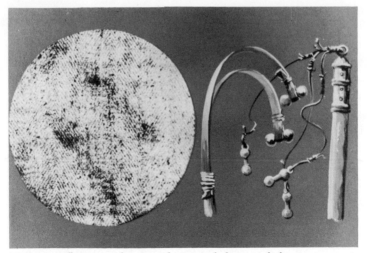

17. Roman flagrums showing the typical design of this instrument of punishment.

There have been various counts made of the number of blows the man on the Shroud received. One researcher estimated that there were close to one hundred fifty blows given to his naked body. It is impossible to be conclusive or categorical on this point as one does not know whether the flagrums used had two or three thongs. The evidence definitely indicates that his hands were tied above his head, that he was naked, and that there were two men wielding the scourges.

An analysis shows that the pattern of blows was so even that it is possible to estimate that there were several inches of difference in the height of the man using a flagrum on the left and the man doing similar scourging on the right.

One may well ask if, in some incredible way, this cloth *was* faked in the Middle Ages by the mind of a genius with a pair of gifted hands, how did this hypothetical forger create such an intricate design? And where did he get the knowledge of a flagrum? Constantine the Great had outlawed crucifixion. In the Middle Ages, there were no dictionaries describing Greek and Roman artifacts. There were no books written about crucifixion in those days; that type of archeological research and the analysis of artifacts came along with the scientific years of the Nineteenth Century. The only libraries in the Middle Ages were in great church centers, and the books were pretty well confined to religious matters. In fact, it can truly be said that nobody knew anything about the details of crucifixion until the research activated by the photograph of the Shroud of Turin.

This next plate (Plate No. 18),shows the back of the head and the shoulders, indicating the large number of lacerations in the back of the scalp and, again, the pattern of blows on the shoulders.

From the head, a long streak that is darker than the area around it can be observed on this plate, falling to about the lower level of the shoulder blades. This has been identified by some sindonologists as a long streak of hair, giving the impression of an unbound pigtail. This is a reasonable hypothesis since the pigtail was common fashion for Jewish men of antiquity, according to research by German scholar H. Gressman. A modern biblical authority, H. Daniel-Rops, explains in his book, *Daily Life In Palestine At The Time Of Christ*, that except on public holidays, Jews wore this pigtail "plaited and rolled up under their headgear."

As one looks at the next picture, (Plate No. 19), which is the magnification of the right shoulder, one thinks naturally of it being the left shoulder because it is on that side as viewed. However, it is important to remember this is the imprint on the cloth resulting from the man lying on the Shroud. On both shoulders there is a marked abrasion and below that, according to doctors who have studied magnified portions of these pictures, there is a bruise over the right shoulder blade.

Dr. Barbet, who wrote *A Doctor At Calvary*, said it reminded him of his experience as a *poilu* in the French

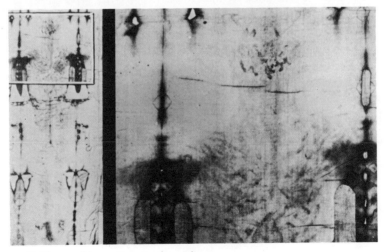

18. Evidence of lacerations in the scalp.

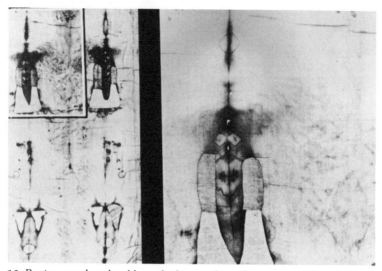

19. Bruise on the shoulder which may have been caused by carrying the cross.

Army during his military training, before he became a physician and surgeon. He assisted in the building of a spur to a military railroad. Occasionally he had to carry heavy ties, and his shoulder would chafe until it was raw. Also when he stumbled, he would get a bruise on his right shoulder blade.

This appears to be a very significant observation. Artists in the Middle Ages liked to portray a huge cross, towering up into the sky, with two smaller crosses on either side for the two thieves, when they pictured the death of Christ. Investigation has shown that nothing could be farther from the truth.

Executions were carried out by Roman soldiers. They were no different basically than other soldiers in any period or any army. They soon found the most practical, quickest and easiest way to do any repetitive job; and they quickly ascertained the simplest way to carry out a crucifixion.

Research has shown that the majority of crucifixions

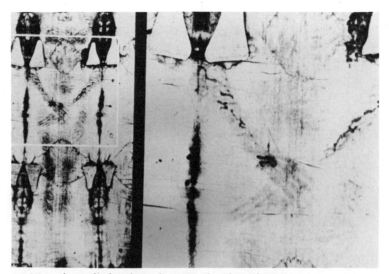

20. Wounds on the hands as shown in the Shroud image.

employed the use of a post, as short as practical, perman-
ently set in the ground. This post had a slot or opening on
the top into which could be fitted a patibulum, thereby
creating a *tau* or T-shaped cross. The patibulum was a short
piece of wood, perhaps six and a half to seven feet long, five
to six inches wide, three to four inches thick, which would
weigh somewhere between fifty and eighty pounds. This, a
man could carry. An entire cross as pictured by the artists
expressing Christian piety in the Middle Ages would be
impossible for a man to carry. The greatest weight lifter in
the history of the Olympic Games could not perform such a
feat. But a patibulum would have caused just such a physical abrasion as those which blot out the marks of the flagrum on the shoulders.

The middle portion of the frontal negative image of the
Shroud of Turin, (Plate No. 20), is perhaps the most significant and important evidence of all, as it is shown magnified
on the right. One notes that there are no thumbs showing.

One observes that there is no hole in the palms of these hands. The wound is where one would locate the wrist, in modern terminology.

Dr. Barbet was fascinated by these two factors. In his position as one of the greatest surgeons of France, he had at his disposal for anatomical research limbs and cadavers, the corpses of paupers. The man on the Shroud has been estimated to be between five-feet, eleven inches and six-feet, one-inch in height. There have been other suggestions, but the great preponderance of scientific opinion lies between these two figures. The weight has been estimated at one hundred and seventy pounds.

Taking these measurements into consideration, Dr. Barbet set up a test to determine whether such a body could be suspended on a cross by nails through the palms. Using pulleys and ropes with amputated arms, he duplicated the exact force such an inert body would exert on nails driven between the bones of the palms. There was not enough strength in the flesh in this area to support one hundred and seventy pounds of dead weight. Obviously, the support of a writhing, suffering, live individual would be much more difficult — there would be far more strain put upon the tender flesh.

Barbet noted that the position of the blood clot on the cloth was roughly over the Space of Destot, in what is now called the wrist. There is no problem semantically here, the wrist is part of the hand, as distinguished from the arm bones, and in the languages from which our accounts of the crucifixion of Jesus were translated, the word "hand" covers what is now called the wrist. The Space of Destot is a miniscule free space where four bones come together, but it is important in the setting of broken wrists. Barbet took a nail and drove it into this point in the wrist; the bones separated without breaking, and he had a firm support that would hold any body. It would seem logical that the Roman executioners would have discovered this fact and used it. But, more significant still, when the nail went through the Space of Destot, the nail scraped, damaged, or severed the trunk of the median, the principal nerve in the arm. The moment this happened, short flexor muscles reacted by tucking the thumb into the palm of the hand.

Now, how could a medieval faker know this? Dr. Barbet's scientific investigation did not produce knowledge of this reaction until 1932. Also, when this nerve is grazed or cut, the fingers curve as the thumbs tuck in. The curving of the fingers is also very noticeable on the Shroud.

As a matter of fact, to repeat, all the artists of the Middle Ages showed a marked lack of understanding and knowledge of this subject. Their painted portrayals of this form of execution are rooted in error. Very few, Van Dyke and Reubens for example, spotted the correct position for the nails in the hands, apparently from viewing the Shroud of Turin, and located them properly. The great majority of painters placed them improperly in the palms.

The blood on the arms is equally significant. A person would be lying with the arms at right angles to the body when the nails were driven through the Space of Destot in both wrists, into the crosspiece. When the patibulum was lifted up to the top of the post, creating a *tau* cross, and the feet were nailed, the body would sag. As soon as a body sags for any period of time, constriction gradually develops in the chest. It affects the muscles in a tetanic fashion, causing painful cramps. When this occurs, the condemned criminal undergoing crucifixion can breathe in, but has great difficulty breathing out.

Accordingly, it is necessary for an individual to stand on his nailed feet in order to breathe. The moment pain forced the resumption of the sagging position, gradual asphyxiation would begin again. The pattern of blood on the arms as portrayed on the Shroud exactly portrays the two angles, with the blood following the course of gravity. With this knowledge, it is easy to understand why the Roman executioners broke the legs of their victims when the punishment was deemed adequate.

Archeologists confirmed Barbet's findings when they unearthed some skeletal remains in one vault of a cemetary in Jerusalem in 1968 — the bones of a man named Jehohanan. His lower legs had been broken, and a spike was still lodged in the heel bones with a bit of olive wood from the cross clinging to it. Barbet would have been delighted to learn that the nail driven into the right arm had left a clearly defined scratch and worn places on the inside of the radius, close to the wrist.

Although the Romans had crucified many thousands of victims — they had put 6,000 to the cross after the Thracian slave Spartacus and his followers revolted in the First Century B.C. — this was the first skeleton of a crucified person ever found. And, as a result, archeologically, as well as medically, evidence from the Shroud's image was proved correct.

The next plate (No. 21) shows the Space of Destot with the nail having parted the bones, so that the opening is clearly seen. One notes that the wrist is part of the hand, the bones in the arm abutt the whole hand.

Plate No. 22 shows where the nail went into the foot of the man on the Shroud, and would apparently be the logical place for any executioner to nail the feet. The *sindon* shows plainly that the left foot was nailed on top of the right.

It is worthwhile to note how so many outstanding artists, after the Fourteenth Century, show the right foot nailed over the left. Reubens is a good example, and there is good evidence that he had seen the Shroud. Of course, however eminent he was in his field, the concept of a reverse image in a negative was not within his scope of comprehension; to his eyes the right had been over the left.

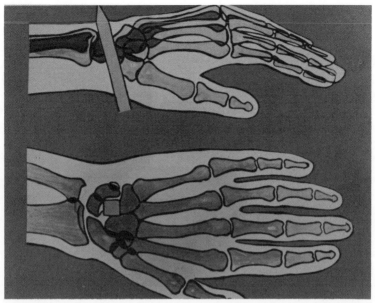

21. Location of the Space of Destot through which nails were driven.

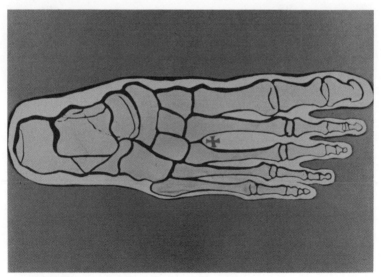

22. Location of the nail in the feet.

One now comes to the question of the fifth wound on the body. Plate No. 23 shows the opening in the side, between the fifth and sixth ribs. General opinion through the centuries was that a body didn't bleed after death, that the blood coagulated. Instead, the right atrium — part of the heart that extends to the right of the breastbone — is always filled with liquid blood. In fact, Dr. Barbet maintained: "The blood remains liquid and never coagulates in a vessel that is still undamaged until dessication or putrefaction sets in." The heart is encased in a sac called the pericardium, and it was this doctor's contention that when somebody dies in agony, depending upon the amount of pain, one will find an additional quantity of hydro-pericardial fluid in this heart sac; just as there is an increase in the urea in the sweat, there is an increase of liquid in this area.

Barbet found in his experiments on cadavers who had just died in great pain that a needle inserted into the

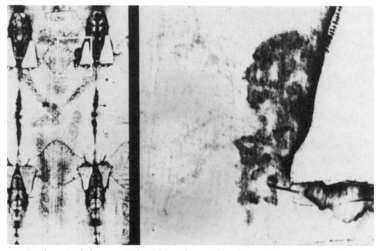

23. Evidence of the wound in the side on the Shroud image.

pericardium would draw out a clear colorless fluid. If the needle was pushed further and penetrated the right atrium he got blood. Also, if a sharp instrument, such as a scalpel, was driven strongly, forcibly, between the fifth and sixth ribs into the heart area, penetrating the right atrium, then both blood and a clear, colorless fluid, would flow. Plate No. 24 gives a diagram illustrating the wound in the side.

It is interesting that in the account of the Crucifixion from the sole recorder, John, it was reported that blood and water flowed. It took a doctor in the mid-1930s to demonstrate that this was accurate reporting. Anatomically, it could have happened just this way, although scientists had questioned this point continually throughout the intervening centuries.

Dr. Gambescia of St. Agnes Medical Center in Philadelphia has advanced another plausible medical support for the the account in the Gospel of John, of blood and water flowing from Christ's side wound. His research has

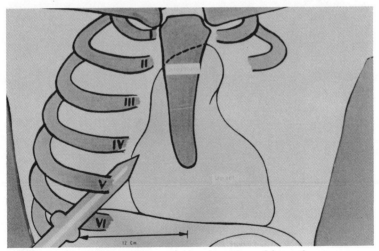

24. Illustration showing the wound in the side and how the spear may have penetrated.

shown that a body which has undergone a severe beating in the chest area will accumulate both blood and clear fluid in the lower chest cavity. Since blood is heavier than water, the water would float on the blood. As a result, a puncture of the chest below the water level will release first blood, then water from the wound. Therefore, whether the wound involved the right atrium, or the lower chest cavity, modern medical scientists have provided convincing support for John's report of the Crucifixion.

Plate No. 25 is a picture portraying Dr. Villandre's concept of the man on the Shroud. Dr. Villandre was a dear friend of Dr. Barbet's. Every point that has been discussed is shown here in this crucifix. A loin cloth has been added so as not to conflict with the social mores of the Twentieth

25. Dr. Villandre's carving of the cruci-
fiction based on Dr. Barbet's medical
evidence.

26. Close-up showing the details of the
crown of thorns.

Century. This is a point that Paul Vignon made much of. He found it impossible to believe that any painter in the Middle Ages could have dared to paint a representation of Christ naked. One notes the distended chest from the tetanic action. One can better understand the two positions in the arms when an individual is standing on his feet and when the body is slumped. Perhaps this beautiful carving makes it clearer why Roman soldiers broke the legs of crucified criminals once they felt their punishment had been sufficient to provide the desired deterrent. After their legs had been broken, it was impossible to stand and breathe and, consequently, suffocation took place.

Plate No. 26 shows the upper portion of Villandre's crucifix, and presents his concept of the crown of thorns; not as an actual crown as portrayed by the artists of the Middle ages, who took it literally. The man on the Shroud must have had a cap of thorns, probably bound around his head as shown here, and in all probability some sadistic soldier jammed a helmet down over his head to make sure that the full effect of this crown of thorns was felt. It would take something of this nature to create the lacerations that are so obvious. This, too, makes sense of the blood trickle on the forehead. The gap referred to earlier could have resulted from such a band, as pictured, holding to the head a cap made of spiny branches.

So, the Shroud's first great medical research pioneer demonstrated half a century ago exactly how this *sindon* portrays the reports in the Bible. All five wounds are graphically illustrated; and with the results of the scourging represented by over one hundred bloody bruises, there is complete agreement between the biblical statements and the physical evidence on this burial cloth. Contemporary investigations by competent pathologists and physicians confirm these initial findings.

Having covered the medical point of view, it is time to return to the historians.

9

THE AGE OF THE SHROUD AND WHERE IT HAS BEEN

DETERMINING THE AGE of the Shroud of Turin has challenged researchers to the present day. The first who gave this topic any intense consideration were Delage and Vignon, as has already been discussed. After the report of their investigation given at the Academy of Science in Paris in April, 1902, there were many claims and counter claims as to the veracity of their work and the soundness of their conclusions.

It has been difficult for people to accept the fact that a piece of cloth could be nearly 2,000 years old. They see how material rots around their own houses in their own lifetimes, and this makes them believe that the same would happen to the linen of ancient days. Yet there are in existence pieces of cloth authenticated as having been found in locked Egyptian tombs existing through the centuries since 1,500 B.C., making them 1,500 years older than the date of the crucifixion.

Another area Vignon pioneered was the study of the way ancient icons and paintings depicted Jesus. Of course, as an accomplished artist, he had no problem realizing how difficult it would be for a painter to try to make a positive picture out of a negative. For that matter, the concept of a negative was completely foreign to anyone until after the

camera was invented, and it certainly was not even suspected in medieval times when the Shroud was first discovered in the possession of the de Charnys.

Not only did Vignon learn that the trend in painting pictures of Christ altered completely in the Fifth Century,
when He began to be shown as a long-haired, bearded man,
instead of a beardless, short-haired youth, but he also found
nearly twenty anomalies in the paintings of the icons which
his trained eye revealed immediately to be elements of a
human face in negative form. By studying these anomalies
it is easy for others who have researched the icons of the
Fifth Century to realize that the face of the icons is the face
of the Shroud.

Dr. Vignon could conceive of other painters throughout
the centuries attempting to paint portraits of Jesus and
using the Shroud of Turin as a basis for it. However, he
knew the painters were not aware that the image on the
cloth, as their eyes saw it, was a negative. Consequently,
they would make many mistakes in attempting to paint a
positive picture from a negative imprint. They would thus
copy certain details of the negative even though these are
peculiarities which no artist would ever consider putting
into a positive face, if he were painting directly from a negative imprint.

Among these are the absence of ears, neck and shoulders;
the forked beard and the two long strands of hair each differently formed; above the nose, a square which does not
have a lid, or top, but is open; a large capital P formed of
the frontal arches and the nose, and more minute peculiarities of the crossbar and the stem of the P; the distorted
appearance of the nose, swollen at the bridge with the
lower part bent to the right; above the open square on the
forehead, a curved transverse stain and a shadow due to a
bruise; the abnormal shading of the swollen right cheek; on
the left cheek, a sheaf of demi-tints in the form of a fan; the

pronounced slanting furrow at the right of the nose; the mustache truncated at both ends and at different angles; the groove between the two halves of the mustache; the formation of the mouth and the shape of the shadow on the bare upper part of the chin.

Naturally, no one piece of work contains all these oddities. Artists would see things in different ways. One has only to look at the negative image to see how vague and diffused it is. It is possible that in some of the pictures the details were copied from prior works of art. Some of them are particularly notable because these minute peculiarities in the Shroud were reproduced so exactly. It has been said by experts in the artistic field that such exactitude could not have been possible unless the painters were actually viewing the Shroud with their own eyes.

In Dr. Vignon's monumental work on the Shroud, which was published in French in 1938 in what appears to be a private edition with a paper cover, he gives a chart. This is superimposed on the negative imprint of the face on the Shroud which details these anomalies—those one would only find in a negative, but not in a positive, and which can be identified in the religious pictures painted after the persecutions ceased.

A discussion of one of these anomalies is sufficient for this study. For example, one may examine the open square, a three-sided box without a top, located immediately above the nose on the forehead. At first glance, it appears to be a crease in the cloth, but it is too remarkably square and accurate at the corners for this to be so. When some scholars have seen this picture, they have suggested that perhaps this was something drawn as a symbol on the forehead by Joseph of Arimathea or Nicodemus, as it is placed directly above the so-called third eye. This line of reasoning suggests that this symbol indicates that the soul has left the body.

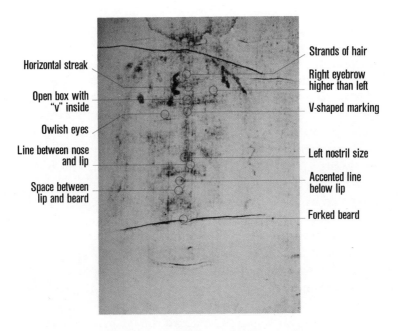

Horizontal streak

Open box with "v" inside

Owlish eyes

Line between nose and lip

Space between lip and beard

Strands of hair

Right eyebrow higher than left

V-shaped marking

Left nostril size

Accented line below lip

Forked beard

Illustration of anomalies noted by Vignon.

Irrespective of such interesting mystical speculation, the picture as shown in Plate No. 6, on Page 19, illustrates all these points perfectly. Observe the open box the artist has drawn in thick lines above the nose. Consider those staring eyes that so obviously reflect what one sees on the negative image of the Shroud. And it is typical of all the icons of that era. This portrait was found in the Roman catacombs and dated from the Sixth or Seventh Century.

It is impossible to overestimate the importance of Dr. Vignon's work in developing his iconographic theory. In modern culture, with humankind's fascination with scientific findings, the significance of his efforts has been all too frequently overlooked, and researchers have gone on evading its inherent implications. Since Vignon's research in this area indicates that the Shroud could be as old as the Seventh Century, the possibility that the man portrayed on it is Jesus of Nazareth has been strengthened considerably. In addition, it is difficult, if not impossible, to explain the similarities in these early icons, except on the basis that they were all copied from one source in this early era. This remarkable research has been practically ignored for nearly fifty years. Our modern culture demanded proof according to scientific standards; this theory could not be evaluated by test tubes, microscopes or new measuring machines. Overwhelming circumstantial evidence and common sense were insufficient for general acceptance at that time.

After the work of Vignon, it was not until 1973 that there was another real step forward that strengthened his evidence. That year, a remarkable criminologist from Switzerland, Professor Max Frei, entered the picture. He was called in to authenticate photographs that had been taken by the panel of scientists who were allowed to investigate the Shroud between 1969 and 1975.

As head of the Zurich Police Scientific Laboratory from 1948 until his retirement in 1972, he investigated important crimes and accidents, including the air crash that killed the U.N. Secretary General Dag Hammarskjold.

On October 4, 1973, Frei noticed the minute dust particles covering the surface of the Shroud. Permission was granted for him to remove some for analysis. He was able to take samples from the Shroud, which was still hanging vertically in the frame that held it during the television exposition of that same year. Frei took samples from the bottom zone to the left and right, and from the side strip.

His method was to press small pieces of clean adhesive tape onto the surface of the linen, then to seal these into plastic envelopes and put them into a satchel he carried with him. Dr. Frei took these specimens back to his laboratory in Zurich where he surveyed the dust collection under the microscope, identifying immediately mineral particles, fragments from hairs and fibers of plants, spores from bacteria and nonflowering plants such as mosses and fungi, and pollen grains from flowering plants. These, of course, were all consistent with the sort of microscopic debris the Shroud could have been expected to accumulate over the centuries. Frei found the pollen to be of the greatest interest, so he began an intensive study of the subject, realizing that identification of the plants from which the pollen had been derived could lead to important deductions about the geographical regions where the Shroud had been. Although they are so small as to be virtually invisible to the naked eye, pollen grains retain their physical characteristics for literally hundreds of millions of years, being immune to almost any form of destruction.

And yet every species of a plant produces a particular pollen which can be distinguished from every other variety, under both the optical microscope and the scanning electron microscope. Also, when viewed under the electron microscope, which produces enlargements of up to 20,000 times or more so that the finest details of the external surface can be studied, pollen grains vary so considerably in physical characteristics that, thanks to careful classification of the different types over the years, it is possible to identify with certainty the precise genus of plant from which any grain has been derived. The special branch of botany called palinology gave Dr. Frei his techniques for this work.

Over a two-year period, Dr. Frei delicately and carefully

studied each pollen grain he had removed from the Shroud, and then cross-matched it against his file of known varieties. His work was made more difficult by the fact that many plants are indigenous to virtually all countries the Shroud might have entered in the course of its travels, and the fact that the same species have often been deliberately planted throughout the area. But three-quarters of the varieties of pollen he found on the Shroud came from plants that grew in Palestine, among them thirteen species which are characteristic of, and almost exclusive to, the Neghev desert and the Dead Sea area, confirming its sojourn there.

Also, according to Professor Frei's research, the Shroud must have been exposed to open air in Turkey, specifically around Anatolia. Twenty of the identified species found came from there, where, interestingly, is to be found the city which once was Edessa. Frei stated, "Modern historians . . . reconstruct the Shroud's travels as follows: Jerusalem, Edessa, Constantinople, Cyprus, France, Italy."

As to the age of the found fragments, Frei points out that the present knowledge does not permit a precise dating due to the fact that the plants represented with their pollens grow even today in the above mentioned areas. We also know from the flora mentioned in the Bible that, in at least the last two thousand years, vegetation in Israel has not undergone any radical change.

Basing his efforts on palinology and his experience as a criminal investigator specializing in the analysis of microfragments, Dr. Frei also studied the possibility of forgery. If this had been done at all, it would have had to have taken place in France prior to 1353—although at that time the study of pollen was not yet known. Still, the forger would have had to acquire from Palestine, with a great deal of effort, a piece of linen carrying dust of that zone. And he would also somehow have had to find a way to obtain pollen from Anatolia and Constantinople.

To the arguments that a *sirocco* or some other great wind storm might have blown pollen from all over the Middle East onto the Shroud at some time when it was being exhibited in France or Italy, Frei agreed that there is no definite way of confirming that this was not possible. However, it is significant that there was no pollen from England found in his research of the Shroud. Surely, if winds had been responsible, some would have blown across the English Channel at some time during these centuries of the Shroud's known existence.

With Vignon's revelations about the face of the Shroud, and Professor Frei's findings in the palinological field, a very strong case has been made for the probability that the Shroud dates to the time of Jesus, and that it originated in the Holy Land. This is not scientific proof that can be reproduced in a laboratory, but it does meet the requirements of common sense as circumstantial evidence.

There is an additional question that is being discussed by today's researchers. It was mentioned earlier that it was the Jewish practice to cover the eyes of the dead with coins. Modern technology was necessary to explain this phenomenon. When photographs were analyzed under microscopes, they showed what to some appeared to be a coin on the right eye. The exciting thing about this is that in this study researchers were convinced they had identified a symbol that is also to be found on coins issued during the reign of Pontius Pilate as Procurator of Judea. It is a symbol like a shepherd's crook with the crook running from left to right as it is viewed.

In 1980, a Jesuit priest, Francis L. Filas, a professor of theology at Chicago's Loyola University, publicly announced that this imprint found on the Shroud of Turin is definitely from a rare coin issued during the time of Pontius Pilate, who passed the death sentence on Jesus Christ. Magnifications of the head show that the rare Pontius Pilate coin— widely used between 27 A.D. and 32 A.D.—show the same misspelling as is on the coin identified as being on the eye of the image on the Shroud. Father Filias said he believes this to be proof the cloth originated around the time and place Christ was crucified.

Father Filas said, in a news release announcing his discovery,

> Imprints of a misspelled Pontius Pilate coin now in existence are the same as imprints of an apparent coin on the right eye of the crucified man's figure on the Shroud of Turin.

> This discovery proves the authenticity, the place of origin, and the approximate dating of the Shroud of Turin beyond reasonable doubt. What makes the discovery so definitive is the fact that a maverick and extremely rare misspelling from the Greek words for "Tiberius Caesar" occurred on both the Shroud pattern and on the coin. Up to now, the "u cai" could only be theorized as a misspelling of a "c" for a "k" in "Tiberius Kaisaros." Now the coin provides concrete proof that the misspelling did exist in the past as it exists today.

He believes this completely excludes the possibility of any forgery of the Shroud.

> No one can reasonably deny that this coin originated in Palestine. This confirms more than ever that the man of the Shroud was a crucified Jew.

There are those students of the Shroud, of course, who deny being able to identify a coin on the right eye of the face. This is typical of the arguments that go on about each phase of *sindon* research, and probably will continue for many years to come, at least until carbon-14 dating is allowed.

In late January of 1982, Dr. Alan D. Whanger made an announcement that may result in more recognition being given Dr. Vignon's iconographic research. Whanger, a psychiatrist at Duke University Medical School, is an amateur photographer who is interested in the Shroud. He photographed and compared four depictions of Christ, dating from the Sixth, Seventh and Tenth Centuries, and compared them for points of similarity in design. These images included: a Sixth Century mosaic from a monastery on Mt. Sinai; a Sixth Century icon from the same monastery; a Seventh Century Byzantine coin issued during the first reign of Justinian II, and a Byzantine coin minted by Constantine VII in 945 A.D.

Using a system of superimposed projection and special filters, Dr. Whanger compared these images with the image on the Shroud of Turin. His results indicated more than 30 points of congruence between the Shroud image and both the mosaic and the Tenth Century coin; 46 points of congruence between the Shroud and the Sixth Century icon, and more than 60 points of congruence between the Shroud image and the coin issued by Justinian II in 685 A.D.

Dr. Whanger's research indicated such exactness between the five images that one is faced with very strong evidence indeed that both artists and both coin designers had to have been copying the Shroud image in their depictions of Christ.

10

OTHER MODERN
SCIENTIFIC RESEARCH
OF THE SHROUD

FOR THIRTY YEARS AFTER Vignon's iconographic research in the 1930s and Dr. Barbet's work during the same era, there was very little definitive study of a scientific nature involving the Shroud.

Then, in 1969, the Archbishop of Turin, on behalf of the exiled King Umberto II, announced that a committee composed primarily of outstanding European scientists had been appointed to investigate the Shroud, and they were allowed to examine it to a degree that had never before been permitted. But when their findings were published in 1976, nothing new or startling had been added to knowledge of the Shroud. The panel of experts was not unanimous in its opinion, for there was still one member who insisted that the image was painted and was a forgery. The majority conclusion, however, was that the cloth "could have come from the area and time of Our Lord," and that it could not be dismissed as a fake relic.

The Right Reverend Jose Cottino, a native of New Bedford, Massachusetts, who was the vice-president of this commission of experts, afterward made the statement that extensive photographic and other tests had been made, that the commission had found no definitive traces of blood, but that they had not discovered anything negative to contradict the belief that this cloth had wrapped the body of Christ. The next scientific examination of the Shroud was largely due to two Americans, John P. Jackson and Eric Jumper. Jumper, an aerodynamics engineer, and Jackson, a physicist, had met at Kirkland Air Force Base in 1974. Both were in their early thirties and devout Catholics and both worked with lasers at the Air Force Weapons Laboratory in Albuquerque, New Mexico. Later these two men were both transferred at the same time to the United States Air Force Academy in Colorado Springs. John Jackson now teaches at the University of Colorado, and Eric Jumper and his family have moved to the Air Force Institute of Technology in Dayton, Ohio.

When Jackson and Jumper first began their research on the Shroud, they made an intensive study of the Enrie photographs. They observed, as Vignon had, that the darkness, or intensity, of each part of the image varies in direct proportion to how far that part of the body would have been from the *sindon* that covered it. The darkest portions would have been closest to the sheet, and the lightest farthest away. They hypothesized that whatever had created the image could have acted at a distance, not just by direct contact.

Early in 1976, Jackson consulted Bill Mottern, an image-enhancement specialist at Sandia Laboratories in Albuquerque, to see if a specific modern machine might be of help in their analysis. Mottern processed the pictures on an Interpretation Systems VP-8 Image Analyzer, a sophisticated instrument designed to convert image intensity to vertical relief, or directly translate pictorial intensity into distance. This machine has been used, for example, to translate photographic images of the Moon and Mars into three-dimensional relief.

Their results startled and amazed them, for they found that the Shroud contains accurate, correctly-proportioned, three-dimensional data. This is something that ordinary photographs and paintings do not have, for they are only two-dimensional. When the image was rotated in order to view the other side, the effect was the same. Details such as the "pigtail" mentioned in Chapter VIII now showed up clearly with a depth that confirmed it could be thick, tightly compressed hair gathered at the back of the neck in the style worn by the early Jews. A separate photograph of the face also showed the same high-relief effect. The men puzzled about unnatural bulges covering the eye areas until they learned about the ancient burial practice of placing coins over the eyes of the deceased.

So with the computer information, Jackson and the others were able to construct a three-dimensional model of the image. This sensational work attracted the attention of other highly qualified scientists, and an organization to study the Shroud informally but scientifically was launched as the Shroud of Turin Research Project (known familiarly as STURP). This group has since attained a membership of some forty sindonologists, many of whom are or were originally stationed at the Los Alamos National Laboratory.

In terms of religion, STURP members belong to various Protestant churches or are Roman Catholics, Jews or even agnostics. However, what they have in common is that each one is the type of person who is challenged by puzzles and "unsolvable mysteries," and is unwilling to believe that any problem can stump him for long. When chemist Ray Rogers joined the organization, he was quoted by Cullen Murphy in "Shreds of Evidence," published by *Harpers* in 1981, as having said, "Give me twenty minutes, and I'll have this thing shot full of holes." That was several years ago.

As this seemed to be a common opinion among members of STURP, they soon began to feel the need to observe and to study the Shroud at first hand, and they took steps toward that end. Of particular assistance in convincing the former king and owner, as well as the Archbishop of Turin, to have a showing with permission to run a series of sophisticated, nondestructive tests, were two priests: American Father Adam Otterbein, C.ss.R., president of the Holy Shroud Guild, and Italian Father Peter M. Rinaldi, S.D.B., his vice president. Fr. Otterbein is a former professor of theology at Mount Saint Alphonsus Redemptorist Seminary in Esopus, New York, and Fr. Rinaldi is a Silesian priest who served for many years in Port Chester, New York, and now serves under the Archbishop of Turin. Fr. Rinaldi first saw the Shroud in 1933 as a young seminarian in the Duomo in Turin, and he witnessed Barbet's identification of the reddish stains on the cloth as blood.

Partially through the efforts of these two religious men, in July, 1978, when the Shroud was once again shown to the public, time was reserved for members of the STURP committee. St. John's Cathedral in Turin was packed to its capacity of 8,000 people, and many thousands more stood outside, as Archbishop Anastasio Alberto Ballestrero of Turin, special master of the Shroud, opened the display after an hour-long devotive mass.

Protected by armed church police, the cloth was displayed in a steel case fronted by bullet-proof glass. It was further guarded by electronic alarms and floodlights blazed down upon it. The case was raised above a ramp in the center of this historic house of worship; and to the crowd streaming in from the bright sunshine outside, looking toward it from the farthest end of the cathedral, it at first gave the appearance of a small movie screen. Behind, and out of view, an array of pipes and dials fed nitrogen into the case, thus preventing oxidation. Other controls assured a constant temperature and humidity level.

Over a period of six weeks, nearly four million people filed past the display, and it was a very moving experience for all who participated. People's reactions varied. One never knew when an individual waiting in line would start to sing a hymn, and then hundreds of others (although of all nations and cultures) would pick up the words and the tune. Some stood weeping as they faced the Shroud. Others stared in blank curiosity. One can readily believe that there were hundreds of thousands of different reactions among the viewers.

This author was present at the two-day conference of the Sindonological Society (*Il Congresso Internazionale di Sindonologia*), which is composed of researchers of the Shroud. This was held at the end of the public viewing. The attendees had a private showing with the opportunity to really see the *sindon* without having to keep up with the moving line.

After the last group of lay viewers had filed past the Shroud, it was taken down and placed in the adjoining royal palace of the House of Savoy. Here it was subjected for five days to exhaustive tests by STURP members, who had shipped to Turin with them sixty-eight boxes of fragile research equipment weighing more than six tons.

Cullen Murphy lists some of their efforts as follows: "They took about eighty photomosaics of the Shroud and processed sixty pairs of X-ray film. They recorded thirty-six X-ray fluorescence spectra, eighty-five infrared-reflectance scans, and eighteen thermograms." Samples were collected with sticky tape from the surface of the linen, just as Frei had done. The resulting samples of fiber and debris and pollen were saved for chemical and microscopic analysis. "A dozen of the threads that had been snipped from the Shroud by Turin's Sisters of St. Joseph in 1973 were transferred to STURP's custody," Murphy says.

Photographs were shot through a microscope, and several hundred rolls of film were used. "It was, in large measure, a carefully-choreographed fishing expedition."

To accomplish all this, these dedicated researchers worked around the clock, sleeping on cots, eating only when they had a spare moment. At the end of this period, the exhausted, but elated, scientists finished their work in Turin. But their major task had only begun. For three years afterward, they spent their spare time analyzing the data acquired. Their results were finally announced in 1981 at their New London, Connecticut, symposium.

11

THE NEW LONDON SYMPOSIUM

THE FORTY-MAN TEAM of the Shroud of Turin Research Project announced the long-awaited results of its intensive three-year study of the Shroud at a three-day conference held at Connecticut College in New London, Connecticut, on October 9, 10, and 11, 1981. Their conclusion: The Shroud is not a forgery. But the group opinion emphasized that there is no concrete proof as to who the figure on the Shroud is.

Attending the conference were some 1,000 participants, including scientists, religious pilgrims and this author. Since obtaining their data in 1978, the members of STURP had used all available means of investigation to determine as many facts as they could, and their ability to declare that the Shroud was not a forgery is a definite step forward in sindonology. They claim, in addition, that they've done some valuable research, and they now know more than they did before. They can explain the chemical ingredients that make up the image of a crucified man, but they cannot explain how that image was formed on the centuries-old linen. In other words, they know what the picture was made of, but they have no idea *how* it was made.

The science team's report said chemical and X-ray tests determined that no pigments, paints, stains or dyes were used to create the image. For a more complete and scientifically detailed report on the STURP research, see L. Schwalde and R. Rogers, "Physics and Chemistry of the Shroud of Turin: A Summary of the 1978 investigation." *Analytica Chimica Acta,* Amsterdam: Elsevier Scientific Publishing Co., 135 (1982), 3-49.

Dr. Alan Adler, a professor of chemistry at Western Connecticut State College, Danbury, Connecticut, announced, "We know the chemistry of the image and the physics of the image. It is absolutely NOT a painting."

Microchemical evaluation has indicated no evidence of any spices or oils on the Shroud. This is not to say that these substances were never on the Shroud, but that there is no trace of them now. The image, instead, was produced by "direct contact with the body," said Joan Janney, a

27. The Shroud was placed on the special table shown so it could be examined from all angles during the five-day intensive study by STURP members. *(Barrie M. Schwortz)*

member of the research team, who is a scientist at the National Science Laboratory in Los Alamos.

> However, while this type of contact might explain some of the features of the torso, it is totally incapable of explaining the image of the face with the high resolution that has been amply demonstrated by photography. . . .
> . . . At the present, this type of solution does not seem to be obtainable by the best efforts of the Shroud team. There are no chemical or physical methods known which can account for the image, nor can any combination of physical, chemical, biological or medical circumstances explain the image adequately.

Dr. Adler reported that the image on the Shroud is that of a "scourged, crucified man. It is not the product of an artist. And the blood stains are composed of hemoglobin." Announcing these findings at the symposium, he was very firm, stating, "It is blood, B-L-U-D, blood," which drew a roar of laughter from the audience. But there is no way to prove whether it is human or animal blood, the strictly objective scientists felt it necessary to declare.

Joseph Gambescia, M.D., of Philadelphia, suggested that because of the position of the blood on the image of the feet and the manner in which the body above was angled on the Shroud, two nails had been used. This is opposed to Dr. Barbet's supposition that only one nail was used, driven between the bones of the feet. The first nail was driven through the right ankle joint; and the second went through both feet, pinning the left foot on top of the right.

The concept that any nails were driven into the upright post of crosses has always been a questionable thesis to this author. If that were done, after three or four executions a post would have been useless. The supply authorities of the efficient Roman army would never have tolerated such waste and additional expense. It is the author's conjecture that in each crucifixion the executioners lashed a disposable block to the bottom of their posts into which one nail was driven through both feet.

The conference was told that the researchers know the body image appearing on the Shroud is nothing more complex than decomposed cellulose, which is the chief constituent of the cell walls of plants, thus becoming an essential part of linen. However, cellulose in linen and other fabrics normally decomposes, but it does not normally decompose in the shape of an anatomically accurate body.

The most important scientific question still to be answered concerning the Shroud is its age. Researchers are waiting for the owner and his advisors to decide whether to allow carbon-14 testing, which could date the cloth, to plus or minus one hundred years. Until recently, this was refused by the religious caretakers of the cloth because too much of the material would have to be destroyed in the testing. But technological advances now open the possibility of carbon-14 testing with tiny amounts of fiber.

"There is no opposition in principal by the bishop for authorizing the testing," said Luigi Gonella of Italy, his representative at the symposium. "He's waiting for a suitable occasion and for proof the tests are reliable, accurate and safe."

When approached just after the conference was over, Douglas J. Donahue, a physics professor at the University of Arizona, which has one of the best carbon-14 facilities in the world, announced that the U. of A. would be honored to use its sophisticated carbon-dating device to determine the Shroud's age. But "As far as I know, we've had no response from the Church," he told the press on October 14, 1981.

The tandem accelerator mass spectrometer delivered to the University in September, 1981, is one of the few machines in the world that would be able to date the

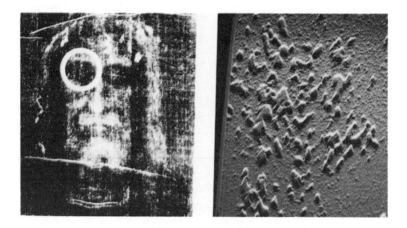

Shroud using a single thread. However, as of the moment this book went to press, the responsible authorities have still not agreed to allow carbon-14 dating, or if they have, this decision has not been announced to the public.

There was also no unanimity in the New London conference about the possibility of there being coins on the eyes of the man on the Shroud. Some members of STURP said they could not see them at all. Others said they were able to identify the one espoused by Fr. Francis L. Filas. No one, however, felt himself able to confirm Fr. Filas' thesis that it is a specific coin of the Pontius Pilate era with the misspelling "Kaisaros." (See Plate No. 28, a, b and c).

Since the conference, Fr. Filas has discovered a second ancient coin with the same rare spelling error that further confirms his theory. He told the Associated Press on November 18, 1981, that he had found, in a department store, a second coin with the same misspelling of the Greek word for "Tiberias Caesar" that occurs on the coin he believes to be on the right eye of the Shroud. He stated that the lettering on the second coin is clearer, and in a different place than letters on the first coin, indicating it is another type of Pontius Pilate coin from a different stamping. He states that this should "close the door" on objections to his conclusions about the first coin.

28. Evidence cited by Fr. Filias in his hypothesis that the coins covering the eyes of the image on the Shroud are Pontius Pilate coins dating from the First Century A.D. **28A** shows the location on the image of the magnified area in B. **28B** shows the letters "UCAI" in the upper left corner. **28C** is a picture of a Pontius Pilot coin.

Papers were read, reports given, and slides shown at the symposium. Immediately after the first session, a photographic exhibit was opened in nearby Groton which was presented by the Brooks Institute of Santa Barbara, California. This is one of the oldest and best schools of photography in the United States. Four of their professors constituted the official photographic team for STURP. Rev. Adam Otterbein, C.ss.R., President of the Holy Shroud Guild, was custodian for this presentation which also contained displays and remained open until mid-December.

One display was a nearly lifesize fiberglass reproduction of a three-dimensional computer-produced model of the Shroud's image unmistakably a rough-hewn statue of a man. According to Vernon Miller, a photographer and chairman of the industrial and scientific department at Brooks Institute, the cardboard and fiberglass model illustrates one of the Shroud of Turin Research Project's more interesting discoveries: that projecting the two-dimensional image of the man which appears on the linen produces a three-dimensional figure.

Computer analyzed photographs give further evidence of the image's three-dimensional properties. "We made these by taking separate exposures of the original Shroud. We assigned an arbitrary color to each density, red, blue or yellow," Miller explained, holding up a bright tri-color photo of the face which appears on the Shroud. The bright colors more sharply define physical features which appear much fainter on normally-exposed pictures of the Shroud's image. Based on earlier research by Jackson and Jumper, and using a VP-8 Analyzer, an instrument which creates a three-dimensional picture from a flat object, the researchers were able to produce a startlingly life-like face from the Shroud image (Plate No. 29).

Fake shrouds were common in the Fourteenth Century, and were sold as religious relics calculated to separate peasants from their limited lucre. Scientists used the analyzer on similar fakes, and distorted images were produced. In a slide presentation, John P. Jackson showed that the three-dimensional images from the fake shrouds were rather flat, and the features were misplaced in contrast to the ones produced from the Shroud.

29. VP-8 Analyzer image of the face on the Shroud of Turin showing the three-dimensional nature of the image. *(Vernon Miller)*

30. Thomas D'Muhalla, left, and John Jackson, right, positioning the Shroud on its examination table. *(Barrie M. Schwortz)*

The question of the fire at Chambery in 1532 was also discussed. The fire was hot enough to melt the silver of the box, but did not incinerate the Shroud. Instead, the molten silver destroyed only a few portions of the cloth — and those were portions away from the image itself, which somehow survived intact, with the exception of the upper arm.

As for the possibility of fraud in the Fourteenth Century, Ray Rogers, a thermal chemist from Los Alamos, said that in that heat any organic pigment on the cloth would have changed color and charred. He considered more than two dozen pigments known to medieval artists, but reported that none had a hope of surviving that heat.

Referring to Vignon's work, Rogers declared that the fire also imperils his vaporgraph theory, for at 200 degrees or more, any organic molecules would decompose and distort the image. There is no evidence of this, however, in the Shroud image.

It is possible, however, that organic molecules could have produced the image and then evaporated, that is, that organic molecules may have caused cellulose degradation and then evaporated before or during the fire of 1532. If this had happened, Vignon's hypothesis is still possible, if the diffusion problem could be resolved.

Other questions regarding this theory include the fact that tests have shown that the diffusion of ammonia would produce a blurry image, not one with the fine resolution that is seen on the Shroud. Also, there would be diffusion of ammonia into the cloth, and the resulting image would therefore not be confined to the surface, as is also the case with the Shroud.

Therefore, the vaporgraphic theory of Vignon still poses

31. Max Frei, right, who did initial research into sources of pollen samples taken from the Shroud, and Ray Rogers examine the cloth. *(Barrie M. Schwortz)*

some unresolved questions which continue to be studied and examined by some scientists. The "hot statue" theory was also discussed. It has been suggested that a forger had heated a statue and then laid the *sindon* on it in such a way that the cloth was scorched in the image of a man. But the members of the panel found that no red-hot statue would scorch evenly. "You can scorch cloth, sure," said Ron London, who works in a M-5 nondestructive-testing group. "You just can't make it look like what we see" . . . on the Shroud.

Ray Rogers added, "The image is too sharp and too uniform for any of the hot statue theories. I incline toward the idea of a scorch."

In an article titled, "Shroud of Mystery," in *Science 81*, Annette Burden writes:

> Finally the Turin team members laid the scorch theory to rest with a technique often used by museums on art treasures. Under ultraviolet light, the scientists watched scorches from the 1532 fire fluoresce reddish as expected, indicating the presence of complex organic compounds produced by high temperatures. But the body image itself did not fluoresce as it would if it too were made up of scorch marks.

But if it was not scorch, what was it? It could have been an unexplained split-second burst of radiant energy from within the folded halves of the Shroud. But a split-second burst of energy, which some believe is proof of the Resurrection, could not be proved by the scientists.

"When we tried to reproduce that all we'd get was a disintegration of threads," said Mrs. Janney. "And you wouldn't get the kind of cellulose degradation you see on the cloth using the flash theory."

However, it should be noted that the body image is located solely on the surface, and only penetrates a few thousandths of an inch into the cloth. Thus, a burst of energy *could* have marked the cloth and produced the image, although scientists still have not proven this possibility using any known source of radiation. Another major theory has been proposed by Samuel Pellicori and is known as the "Latent Image, Cellulose Degradation" theory. According to this,

> Natural skin substances, or applied burial ointments, were transferred to the Shroud by direct contact with the body. These materials acted as the catalysts necessary to accelerate the degradation of cellulose at those points where contact was made. With the passage of time, an image was formed. The original substances have disappeared, whether through washing or by being consumed in the reaction.

Pellicori has substantiated his theory by impregnating linen with different substances, such as perspiration and oils, and air baking it in an oven to simulate aging. His results are very similar to the Shroud body image when examined with a spectroscope.

One problem with the theory is that if the face was produced by direct contact, one would expect distortion in the image. However, very little distortion can be seen in the image of the man on the Shroud.

Therefore, while Pellicori's hypothesis might explain some of the features of the torso that came into contact with the Shroud, it does not explain how the image of the face was produced with such high resolution. Also, deep features of the face, such as the eye sockets, would not be touched by a stiff linen cloth.

A deputy medical examiner for Los Angeles County, Dr. Robert Bucklin, has professionally encountered all the wounds suffered by the man on the Shroud, although never "all on the same body." In order to acquire first-hand experience he once suspended himself from a crucifix, using leather thongs. He says the pain was all but unbearable as his deltoid and pectoral muscles went into spasms and left him unable to breathe. "I think without question we have a crucified person here with the cause of death congestive cardiac failure," he said.

Speaking for the team, Dr. Eric Jumper, now president of STURP, said, "What we've all done is prove a lot of negatives. We know what's on the cloth, but we don't know how it got there."

In summary, Dr. Bucklin's own personal belief, apart from his scientific conclusions, is that, "Nothing produced by the team prohibits the concept of resurrection forming the image."

There will be other researchers. Other scientific minds will be intrigued by this centuries-old mystery and give their expertise and energy in attempts to add to humankind's knowledge of the Shroud. One of the most recent recruits, John A. DeSalvo, Ph.D., a biophysicist and physiologist of St. Paul, Minnesota, has presented a fresh concept.

In his work, Dr. DeSalvo notes that when certain plant matter, such as a leaf, is placed in a book and left undisturbed for many years, a faint, sepia-colored image is formed on both the upper and lower sheets of paper. This image is called a Volckringer pattern. These patterns were first studied by Jean Volckringer at St. Joseph's Hospital in Paris in the 1940s.

Dr. Barbet (see Chapter VIII) had also noticed that these sepia images closely resembled the image on the Shroud and that considerable detail is visible in Volckringer patterns, as in the Shroud image. In addition, the Volckringer patterns produced are a negative and, when photographed, produce a positive image similar to Pia's discovery of the negative nature of the Shroud image.

DeSalvo has done the first quantitative color comparison between the Shroud image and Volckringer patterns using a spectrophotometer, and he has found specific Shroud body areas to be almost identical to a typical Volckringer pattern. In addition, neither Volckringer patterns nor the Shroud image fluoresce under ultraviolet light. It should also be noted that both the linen of the Shroud and the paper involved in Volckringer patterns have a high content of cellulose.

Pellicori proposed that after the body was removed from the Shroud the image did not appear until considerable time had passed, which seems to be true of Volckringer patterns as well. In addition, the Volckringer patterns show the plant in its natural, living state, rather than dried up.

However, Volckringer patterns differ from the Shroud image in that they are not a surface phenomenon, but penetrate into the paper.

32. Volckringer patterns formed by a fern leaf.

DeSalvo's theory is called the "Revised Vaporgraphic—Direct Contact Hypothesis," and involves some parallels to Volckringer patterns. Volckringer patterns are formed when acids are transferred to the paper, causing cellulose degradation or modifications of the cellulose molecules, thereby producing an image after a period of time. The image appears because light is reflected differently from the portions of the cloth where the cellulose degradation takes place. The essential difference between Pellicori's work and DeSalvo's at this point is the hypothesis that acids are the main transferring agents in both the case of the Shroud and the Volckringer patterns.

DeSalvo's theory notes that lactic acid is one of the plant acids that would be involved in Volckringer pattern production on paper. Human perspiration contains a certain amount of this acid, in addition to water, sodium chloride, urea, potassium and other substances. It is likely that a person who had been tortured and crucified would have sweated profusely and produced significantly larger amounts of lactic acid. This, then, could have been the transferring agent involved in producing the image on the Shroud.

However, DeSalvo goes on to note that his research leads him to conclude that another process must also have been involved in order to produce those parts of the Shroud image located in areas where the body and Shroud did *not* touch.

It is possible that the linen was originally stiff, similar to a starched shirt, and that it gradually sagged closer to the body as it became softer in the tomb. This has been proposed by John German, a member of STURP, and would account for how the cloth got close enough to produce an image with high resolution by the vertical diffusion of lactic acid.

DeSalvo explains the three-dimensional nature of the image as follows: as expected, the lactic acid concentration on the cloth would be less in areas farther from the cloth, and greater in areas closer to the cloth. The greater the lactic acid concentration, the more cellulose degradation would occur. Therefore, the intensity of the image produced would vary with the cloth-to-body distance. And, since the cloth-to-body distance would be assumed to be extremely small, a high resolution of image would result, not a blurred one.

An additional study which shows the similarity between the shroud body image and Volckringer patterns is three-dimensional reconstruction. Plate 32A shows a 3-D reconstruction of a Volckringer pattern using a Log E/ISI EARTHVIEWS System. DeSalvo enlisted the help of David Koger from LogE/Interpretation Systems Inc. in Kansas to perform this reconstruction.

However, the body image, as stated above, is a surface phenomenon. If the lactic acid theory is correct, why didn't

32A. Three dimensional reconstruction of Volckringer pattern.

the acid diffuse into the cloth, as is the case with Volckringer patterns? One possible explanation would be that the lactic acid was confined to the surface by the absorbency of the cloth.

A study done by John Tyrer for the Manchester England Chamber of Commerce Testing House and Laboratories indicates that the

> Comparatively closely set structure of the linen may not be immediately absorbent of water, let alone the more viscous liquids draining from a corpse. The water stains on the Shroud that were apparently produced in extinguishing the Chambery fire do not suggest a high and rapid absorbency.

This may explain why lactic acid was confined to the surface. Then, over a period of time, the lactic acid caused cellulose degradation. The lactic acid was eventually removed, either by washing or evaporation, so by the time of the 1532 fire, no organic molecules were present on the Shroud, only the result, that is, the image produced by cellulose degradation.

This may also explain why the hair leaves an impression on the cloth. In the scalp, there are apocrine sweat glands associated with hair which produce a fatty sweat containing unsaturated fatty acids, urea, lactic acid and other substances. The hair of the man on the Shroud was probably drenched in sweat containing these acids. Evaporation of these acids, or direct contact with the cloth, would also have produced cellulose degradation after many years.

The image of the coins over the eyes reported by Fr. Filas might also be similarly explained. For example, it is possible that the eye sockets filled with sweat and slightly coated the coins. If this happened, the diffusion of the acids in the sweat may have produced the markings of the coins reported on the Shroud. Another possibility is that someone may have handled the coins and his sweaty hands left some perspiration on the coins.

One additional problem that still needs to be resolved is the uniformity of shading of the fibers on the Shroud. The straw yellow fibers all have the same intensity of color, yet some areas of the image are more intense than others. The density of the image is determined by the concentration of colored fibers in a given area. A similar example can be seen in the printing of photographs which involves a pattern of tiny dots. The darkness or lightness of the image is caused by the density, or number, of dots used, not by differences in shading between the individual dots.

Therefore, Dr. DeSalvo's theory attempts to resolve a number of previously "sticky" issues regarding the Shroud image by indicating that two mechanisms might have been involved in producing it: a direct contact process; and a molecular diffusion process involving lactic acid diffusing through short distances to the cloth, based on the assumption that lactic acid was the substance responsible for the production of the image through cellulose degradation.

This recent research, combined with the work of earlier scientists such as Barbet and Vignon, has provided a variety of possible explanations of the phenomenon of the Shroud image, as well as a basis for continuing research along several lines. By their very nature, these scientific investigations have been limited to the physical evidence, the complete explanation of which may still be beyond the present limits of scientific inquiry.

In the Afterword, this subject will be considered from a personal, and other than strictly scientific, viewpoint.

AFTERWORD

PERSONAL REFLECTIONS
ON THE RESURRECTION

NOW THAT SOME OF THE FORMERLY skeptical
STURP members who went to Turin have openly
stated that what they see on the Shroud might
indicate the possibility of the resurrection of Jesus, science
and faith are closer on this subject than they have been
since the inception of modern rationalization nearly two
hundred years ago. It cannot be said that a marriage has
been consummated between these two aspects of humankind's thinking, but one might speculate that they are near
to a betrothal.

At the exhibition in Groton put on by the Brooks
Institute after the Shroud of Turin Research Project
Symposium, the crowds who poured in to see the displays
and photographs made the focal point of their interest very
apparent: the majority believed the image of the Shroud is
that of the Nazarene and they wanted the scientists to say
so. It could be summed up as, "Tell us it's Jesus." This, of
course, is not possible, even were carbon-dating tests to
verify that the Shroud comes from His time. There is no
way of *proving* that the image is that of the crucified
Founder of Christianity. No matter how overwhelming,
circumstantial evidence is not proof in the scientific sense. It
may be sufficient to get a verdict of positive identification in

a court of law, but it does not meet the demands of absolute verification such as provided by a microscope or a test tube.

Nonetheless, despite Dr. Jumper's statement to the effect that STURP's work resulted in more negatives than positives, the major doubt was dispelled. The majority opinion of the team is that no mythical genius of the Middle Ages created the image on the Shroud by any means known to science. Thus, the preponderance of detail developed or confirmed by them could strengthen Christian belief.

Over the centuries, atheists have challenged biblical writings and maintained that the Galilean is a myth. But after the findings of this organization, it would be a Herculean task to prove that the man on the Shroud is *not* Jesus: a rational effort to do so would face odds of millions to one.

Two of STURP's findings strongly indicate the probability of resurrection, and thus support this concept. The image plainly shows a crucified man in *rigor mortis;* yet there is no sign of decomposition, so it is obvious that the man on the Shroud was not in the burial cloth for an extended period of time. Further, the body shows that there was bleeding from wounds that exactly match the accounts in the Gospels of the injuries suffered by the Master. In places, the flow of blood was heavy and penetrated the cloth. There was obviously contact between these bloody areas and the burial linen. One would expect there to be indications of adherence at these points, but this is not the case. The extensive research shows that the blood clots were undisturbed, retaining their unbroken form. Nobody could have removed the body from its linen wrapping without smearing the blood no matter how carefully it was attempted. And, anyway, why should thieves leave the Shroud if the purpose was to steal the body? They would have covered the corpse with it in order to carry it.

How did the body get out of the cloth? Turning to the Bible, it would be far simpler if one could quote an account from the four Gospels which would include in chronological order the events of the first Easter. That is not possible. There is too much variance in the reports, although none casts doubts on the primary issue of the Nazarene rising from the dead. So let the description given in St. John present the bibilical position. John 20:1-10 gives his account of the events as follows:

Mary Magdalene arrived at the tomb before daylight and saw that the stone was removed from the entrance. Apparently assuming that the body was no longer in the tomb, Mary ran and informed Peter and John, who hurried to check her statement. John, who was younger, arrived first, but waited for Peter, who, the account says, entered before him. Then we have the statement which adds another dimension to the mystery: "He saw and believed. For they did yet not understand from the scripture that He had to rise from the dead."

It has been suggested that the only logical explanation for this statement from John is that he and Peter saw the Shroud lying in the shape of a body, but empty. If this conjecture is correct, it would eliminate any question of transmutation —the body being instantly changed from mortal flesh to a divine substance—because the spiritualized body would just have replaced the mortal body. But then the divine body would have had to extricate itself without disturbing the Shroud's shape. If the burial cloth were lying in disarray like a bed from which someone had just arisen, there would be no basis for believing He had resurrected from the dead. So what would have convinced Peter and John?

John's gospel, in his twentieth chapter, verses nineteen and twenty-six, refers to the two occasions when Jesus came to His disciples when "the doors were locked." To do this, He had to pass through a solid wall or door. How was this accomplished? This biblical statement is either false, or it really happened. How could a body, one that would be touched and probed by the doubting Thomas, pass through a solid wall or locked door? Wouldn't it be reasonable that in some manner that defies a rational explanation the body was dematerialized on the outside of the room and re-formed on the inside? Perhaps this is also the way the corpse left the *sindon*.

A scenario based on John's brief account of the events of the early morning of the first Easter might go as follows:

Peter is wearing the mourning black and, according to custom, has rent his garments. The younger, more agile, disciple precedes him as they hurry up the side of the hill to the tomb, which faces east. They find the stone, which is shaped like a plate, rolled back into its slot. They are both thinking, "Why? Who has stolen the Master's body?" They hesitate and peer in before stepping inside. In the early sunlight shining in from behind them, they can see the folded napkin that had held his chin, now located on the right of the sepulcher. They step within and reel back in astonishment. On the left, there is the couch carved out of the rock where the tortured and crucified body had been laid. It should be dark where the sun's rays do not reach it, but instead it is lighted. The Shroud is just where Jesus had left it, in the shape of His body. On it is His death image, freshly created. And the cloth is still glowing with a radiance that lights the rock-hewn burial chamber. They pray and give thanks, for now they understand the meaning of the scriptures that He must rise from the dead — that he has "rebuilt this temple in three days." (John 2:20,21)

If this conjecture is accurate, it leads to the problem of what effect such a movement through the linen would leave on it. Again science, which can put men on the Moon, cannot help us here; this can only be approached on the basis of faith, or rational, reasoning inquiry. What form of energy is involved, then? Was this a different manifestation of applied atomic energy? It is now known that every atom in matter contains energy. With modern Kirlian techniques of photographing the luminescence, or aura, around objects, it is now possible to see the energy that somehow radiates from all things.

Throughout the centuries, likenesses of Jesus, and others to whom saintly powers were attributed, have shown halos around their heads. Normal human eyes cannot see such emanations, and it is logical for questing minds to wonder about the source of this concept. Can this belief be linked to the Transfiguration on the Mount as recorded in the Gospels? In the descriptions are:

"... the appearance of His countenance was altered, and His raiment became dazzling white," Luke 9:29

"... and He was transfigured before them, and His garments became glistening, intensely white ..." Mark 9:2,3

"And He was transfigured before them, and His face shone like the sun." Matt. 17:2

Are these portraying a power that could have been responsible for the negative three-dimensional image on the Shroud of Turin? Some STURP members described this power as best they could: "It was an unexplained split-second burst of radiant energy from within the folded halves of the Shroud," they said. And, "a burst of radiant energy—light, if you like."

After the first real attempt at investigation in Paris at the turn of the century, Dr. Paul Vignon concluded that the image was formed by the action of carbonate of ammonia fumes on the aloetin in the ancient Jewish burial fluid. This theory was approved by his mentor, Dr. Yves Delage, who announced at the conclusion of his presentation on Dr. Vignon's research to the Academy of Sciences, in 1902, "Gentlemen, you are looking at the face of Christ on the Shroud of Turin."

Dr. Vignon, however, always maintained that his findings constituted a theory, not scientific proof. In his statement to this learned society, Dr. Delage was combining legal and scientific positions from the biblical reports and chemical findings. He certainly had a strong case on the basis of circumstantial evidence, but not by the standards of exact science.

The highly trained specialists of STURP, using the latest technical equipment in their research between 1978 and 1981, concluded that there is no trace of burial spices on the Shroud. Vignon's vaporgraphic theory thus has been labeled as incorrect, but how would the scientists know this if all the evidence had been burned away by a form of energy that their disciplines cannot yet define?

To explain the scriptural references to aromatic, vegetable substances that were used as preservatives, it has been suggested that they were packed loosely around the body and hence traces could not be expected to be found on the *sindon*. In the first studies in this area, Dr. Rene Coulson, the friend and associate of Vignon, did extensive research to determine the constituents of the Jewish burial fluid. The vaporgraphic theory was based on his findings: olive oil into which was blended myrrh and aloes, as prescribed by Moses.

The King James version of John 19:39 says that Nicodemus provided, "a mixture of myrrh and aloes, about a hundred pounds weight." There is, however, a significant difference in the Lamsa version regarding the quantity of spices.

The late George M. Lamsa translated the *Peshitta*, the Aramaic bible referred to earlier. His knowledge of Aramaic and its idioms, learned as a child in Assyria, contributes new insight into his translation of the Gospels. This results in small, but significant variations from previous translations, which were based on Greek or Latin texts.

For example, he translates John's gospel: 19:39 and 40, as follows.

> And there came also Nicodemus who at first had come to Jesus by night: and he brought with him a mixture of myrrh and aloes, about a hundred pints. So they took away the body of Jesus and bound it in linen cloths with the spices, according to the custom of the Jews in burial.

The use of the description "one hundred pints" certainly implies that the powdered aromatic preservatives were in a liquid base. This again brings into focus a major element in Dr. Vignon's vaporgraphic theory as opposed to the use of the loose spices hypothesis. Why should there be a variation from the Jewish burial procedures by such prominent members of the Sanhedrin as Joseph of Arimathea and Nicodemus? Especially since this governing body of the Hebrew faith at that time could be roughly compared to the College of Cardinals in Catholicism.

If the Shroud was saturated with olive oil in which the two spices were blended, what would be the effect on it of a burst of spiritual energy? What scientist can measure or describe the effects of the action of the Holy Spirit as part of the resurrection process on such a linen cloth? Did the power that created a negative photographic likeness on this *sindon* at the same time fix the organic burial preservatives so that it has survived handling over the centuries without leaving a trace of vegetable matter on it? These are all questions that science is not presently equipped to answer.

When one reflects on science's inability to explain how the image was formed, one is faced with such imponderable questions. There are no answers, only the weight of massive, circumstantial evidence that indicates a spiritual origin. Wouldn't this make any conclusions as to how the image was formed based on modern scientific knowledge very questionable?

Even with so many indications pointing toward the authenticity of this *sindon*, there are persons, particularly those who have not studied it carefully, who will maintain that it is a fake. As Dr. Delage wrote more than seventy-five years ago, "If it were Sargon, Achilles or a pharoah, there would be no question. It is the fact that it is the Founder of Christianity that causes men's minds to boggle." The scientists of STURP have stated emphatically that the Shroud is not a fake. Acceptance of their explanations requires another type of faith: belief based on the incredible feats of science.

There is also, however, another way of evaluating this question of authenticity or forgery simply by applying the time-proven principles of common sense. Let us reflect on the known facts.

There is an unbroken chain of evidence for the existence of this burial cloth since it was first displayed in Lirey, so it must have been created prior to the Fourteenth Century. On a practical basis, if we ignore the evidence provided by Vignon with his iconographic research, what problems would have faced an artist in the Middle Ages who sought to fake this likeness?

The first requirement would have been obtaining a *sindon* manufactured in the Middle East with fossilized pollen on it from the Holy Land and Turkey. Then, at a time when photography had not yet been invented and the concept of a negative was unknown, he would have had to portray a photographic reversal using some substance that shows no evidence of paint or dye. Further, he would have had to have painted this likeness so that it is three-dimensional—which is not true of ordinary photographs or paintings. And he would have to have painted it so that the closer one got to it the less one saw.

Somehow, the creator of this image would have to have acquired details of the technique of crucifixion, even though no one had been executed in that fashion for approximately one thousand years (and there were no books available on the subject). In order to conform to the biblical account of Jesus' death on the cross, he would have had to display the medical knowledge of a modern surgeon. This would have required the use of fresh blood to create factual patterns of flow on the head and arms before it coagulated. To match the Gospel accounts of the scourging he would have had to include in this likeness more than one hundred bloody bruises from the use of an obsolete Roman flogging implement. In addition, the pattern of the blows would have had to indicate that there were two executioners of different heights. But the Gospel accounts do not mention two executioners, of slightly different heights. So where would this alleged forger have received the idea? Dr. Vignon wrote that no artist could paint such a pattern. Also, the creator of this likeness would have had to incorporate such details as the coins on the eyes that cannot be seen without modern magnification.

In addition to all this, this postulated all-knowing genius who was attempting to produce a forgery would have had to have such spiritual insight that he could invest the magnificent face with a serene majesty, yet also have the audacity to portray a completely nude figure of the Christ at a time when the social mores made such a representation unthinkable.

Common sense indicates that the requirements to produce the Shroud of Turin by human means would have demanded abilities that no man of that time could have possessed. A spiritual resurrection is, therefore, far more logical and likely.

Christianity started with a group of simple people in a conquered province on the far outskirts of the Roman Empire. With the death as a criminal, by crucifixion, of its leader and teacher Jesus, this small cult would surely have soon faded into oblivion but for one thing—the belief in His resurrection. This belief was at the root of the growth of Christianity to a place of dominance in the Western World. Now, in a culture dominated by science and materialism, we have been presented with the first material evidence of the possibility that the Nazarene actually rose from the dead.

Summary of the Significance of the Shroud

Understanding of the Shroud of Turin has greatly advanced since Pia first pulled that glass plate from his developing tank in 1898, thereby adding another enigma to a subject that had been a riddle for centuries.

At that time, knowledge of the Shroud was limited to a small portion of Europe. But today, interest is worldwide, and the subject receives continuing attention from all forms of the media.

There is still controversy regarding whether this cloth is a fake or a genuine *sindon*. However, the positive findings in the latest scientific report should dispel doubts in this area. Even if carbon dating places origin of this linen winding sheet in the era of Jesus of Nazareth, there will still be a minority that the overwhelming evidence—scientific, circumstantial, artistic, and logical—will fail to convince.

For reasoning Christians, irrespective of their denominations, two questions take shape in the mind: What is its purpose and what does it mean to us? Once more, there are no empirical answers. God's purpose could be to inspire us to the same thinking that resulted in early Christianity. Jesus' teachings were followed because there was such a strong belief that He rose from the dead.

The research into the likeness of Jesus provides a possibly helpful bonus for those who are convinced of the Shroud's genuineness.

Jesus said, "God is spirit" (John 4:24). It has been difficult for us to believe in a singular God, a God of spirit, one not shaped in a visual image: hence the vast quantity of anthropomorphic portrayals to be found.

Jesus also said, "He who sees Me has seen the Father" (John 14:8).

It is now possible to visualize the Nazarene through the evidential portrait that has been developed. The development of this portrait is discussed extensively in a monograph available from the publisher. This could personalize the Spirit or the spiritual for us. It is a matter of individual preference.

Has God's protective hand guided the Shroud during its centuries of vicissitudes? Through this faded linen with its faint image, is it God's purpose to stimulate a stronger interest in Jesus' teaching, based on the implications of His rising from the dead? Does it constitute a message of love from God?

There are many possible answers to these questions, each a matter of personal thinking and belief, and each reader must decide on the basis of his or her conscience. As for this author, the answer is a resounding, "Yes".

APPENDIX

This evidential portrait of Jesus, by artist Ris Phillips, is based on the measurements of the image on the Shroud of Turin, as well as First Century A.D. reports relating to Jesus' appearance and coloration. The portrait was commissioned by Frank O. Adams in 1971.

Full color reproductions of this evidential portrait, and *The Face Of Jesus*, a monograph by Frank O. Adams which outlines the development of the portrait and the research upon which it is based, can be ordered from Patrick Walsh Press, 2206 S. Priest, #105, Tempe, Arizona 85282.

The evidential portrait of Jesus by Ris Phillips.

CHRONOLOGY OF THE SHROUD*

Circa 27/32   Pontius Pilate coin, researched by Fr. Filas, minted.

Circa 30-33   Crucifixion of Christ (Addai or Thaddaeus travels to Edessa, Shroud given to Abgar V.)

Circa 57   Manu VI, Abgar's son persecutes Christians (Shroud hidden above Edessa's Western gate).

Circa 312   St. Helena (Mother of Constantine) sees Shroud in Jerusalem.

Circa 330   Roman Emperor Constantine converts to Christianity and declares it the official religion of Rome. This marks the end of persecution of Christians.

Circa 360   Julian the Apostate allows belief in all faiths.

Circa 400   Major change in the depiction of Jesus's likeness in paintings, sculptures and carvings, icons, now resembling Shroud.

Fifth/Sixth   Antonius Placentunus and St. Nino purported
Century   to have seen Shroud.

525   Shroud discovered in Western gate of Edessa during rebuilding following massive flood damage.

---

* This chronology includes dates from various theories (sometimes contradictory) of the Shroud's location over the centuries.

544	Evagrius writes of Mandylion miraculously preserving Edessa from Persian attack.
590	Byzantine icon made in likeness of Shroud (45 points of congruence).
631	St. Braulion, Bishop of Saragossa reports on Shroud.
670	Arculph sees and kisses Shroud in Jersalem.
692	Gold coin minted resembling Shroud (60 points of congruence).
Circa 700	Edessa surrenders Mandylion to Monophysite Athanasius Bar Gumayer. Shroud mentioned or seen by English Theologian Venerable Bede, St. Willibald, Emperor Baldwin, St. John Damascene.
944	Mandylion arrives in Constantinople. Housed in Pharos Chapel.
Circa 1100	Over 20 reports of Shroud amongst them: William of Tyre, Alexius of Comenos, Peter the Deacon. Two Catalogues made by Pilgrims to Constantinople.
1130	Pope Stephen III refers to Mandylion.
1185	Templecombe Center built by Templars.
1204	Robert De Clari describes seeing Shroud at My Lady, St. Mary of Blanchernae.
1247	Crusaders sack Constantinople and Shroud disappears. Shroud in catalogue of empire.
1314	Grand Master Jaques De Molay and Geoffrey De Charnay, last of Templars, burnt at stake in Paris. The latter was possibly a protector of the Shroud.
1353	Geoffrey De Charny (relation to namesake uncertain) obtains rent from King John the Good for Church of Lirey.
1356	Shroud being shown in Lirey Chapel. Medallions struck bearing arms of Geoffrey De Charny and Jeanne De Vergy.

1418	Marguerite De Charny ordered to surrender Shroud after the death of her first husband, Jean De Baufremont at Agincourt. Marguerite remarries to Count Villersexel, Count De La Roche.
1453	Marguerite gives Shroud to Duke of Savoy.
1478	Queen Anne of Britanny makes pilgrimage to see Shroud.
1512	Ducal church built at Chambery houses Shroud.
1516	Sainte Chapelle of Holy Shroud built.
1532	Fire disfigures Shroud.
1534	Poor Clare Sisters repair Shroud.
1578	Shroud moved to Turin.
1694	Shroud placed in Royal Chapel, Turin.
1868	Princess Clothilde adds red silk backing.
1898	Secundo Pia photographs Shroud and discovers the negative nature of the image.
1901	Chevalier condemns Pia.
1902	Yves Delage announces Shroud is the burial cloth of Jesus at French academy of Sciences.
1931	Exposition of Shroud for 21 days. Photographs repeated and Pia exonerated.
1932	Dr. Barbet's research into medical aspects of figure on the Shroud.
1933	Public exposition of The Shroud of Turin.
1938	Dr. Vignon publishes his research and vaporgraphic hypothesis.
1963	"A Doctor at Calvary," by Dr. Barbet, reports medical findings relating to the Shroud.
1969	Panel of scientists examine and photograph Shroud.
1970	Evidential portrait of Jesus based on Shroud commissioned by Frank Adams.
1973	Max Frei begins pollen research.
1976	1969 team issues report on Shroud.

1977	STURP team researches Shroud of Turin.
1978	400th anniversary of Shroud, in Turin. Pope John XXIII gives permission for exposition. Pope John Paul I elected same time as opening and dies before end of exposition.
1980	Fr. Filas publishes research tying Shroud to Pontius Pilate coins.
1981	STURP symposium in New Long, Conn.
1982	Dr. Whanger reports on research into coins, icons, and Shroud.

BIBLIOGRAPHY

Barbet, P., M.D., *A Doctor At Calvary*. Garden City, NY; Image
Books, 1963.

Brent, P., and Rolfe, D., *The Silent Witness*. London: Futura
Publications, 1978.

Cheshire, Leonard, *Pilgrimage to the Shroud*, New York, McGraw Hill
Book Co., 1956.

Daniel-Rops, H , *Daily Life In Palestine At The Time Of Christ*. London:
Weidenfeld, 1962.

Filas, F., *The Dating Of The Shroud Of Turin From Coins of Pontius Pilate*,
Monograph, Cogan productions division, Youngtown, Arizona,
1980.

Humber, Thomas, *The Sacred Shroud*. New York: Pocket Books,
1963.

McEvoy, W. V., *The Death-Image of Christ*, Victoria: Holy Name
Headquarters.

McMahon, W.D., Ed.,*The Archko Volume*. Grand Rapids, Michigan:
Wm. B. Eerdman's Publishing Company.

Rinaldi, P., *It Is The Lord*. New York: Warner Books, 1972.

_____,*When Millions Saw The Shroud*. New Rochelle, NY: Don
Bosco Publications, 1979.

_____, *The Holy Shroud*. New Rochelle, NY: A Don Bosco
Pamphlet, 1978.

Savio, Mons. P., *Richerche Storiche Sulla Sindone*. Societa Editrice Internazionale, Biblioteca Del Salesianum, 1957 Page 191.

Solaro, Sanna Gammaria, *La S. Sindone*, Torino, Itality, Vincenzo Bona, 1901.

Sox, D. *The Image On The Shroud, Is The Turin Shroud A Forgery?*. London: Unwin Paperbacks, 1981.

Stevenson, D., and Habermas, G., *Verdict On The Shroud*. Michigan: Servant Books, 1981.

Stevenson, K., Ed. *Proceedings Of The 1977 United States Conference Of Research On The Shroud Of Turin*. Bronx, NY: Holy Shroud Guild, 1977.

Tyrer, John, "Notes Upon The Turin Shroud As A Textile." *General Report and Proceedings of the British Society For The Turin Shroud*. Autumn 1979 - Summer 1981.

Vignon, Paul, *The Shroud of Christ*. New Hyde Park, N.Y.: University Books, 1970.

Volckringer, J., *Le Probleme des Emprientes Devant La Science*. Paris: Libraire Du Carmel, 1942.

Walsh, John, *The Shroud*. London: W.H. Allen, 1964.

Wilson, Ian, *The Shroud of Turin*, Garden City, N.Y.: Doubleday & Co., Inc., 1978.

Wilcox, R.K., *Shroud*. New York: Macmillan, 1977.

Wuenschel, E.A., *Self Portrait Of Christ*. Bronx, NY: Redemptorist Fathers of New York, Holy Shroud Guild.

_____, *The Holy Shroud*. Esopus, NY: Holy Shroud Guild.

Zugibe, F., *The Cross And The Shroud*. McDonagh and Co., Creskill, New Jersey, 1981.

Periodicals

Beckstead, L., "The Men of the Shroud," *Frontier Magazine*. The Webb Co., February, 1981.

Bortin, V., "Science and the Shroud of Turin," *Biblical Archeologist*. Vol. 43, No. 2, p109-117, Spring, 1980.

Burden, A., "The Shroud of Turin," *Santa Barbara Magazine.* Vol. 6, No. 4, p40, Winter 1980.

_____, "The Shroud of Mystery," *Science 81.* Vol 2, No. 9, p76-83, November, 1981.

Cook, C., "Coin of the Shroud of Turin," *Coinage Magazine.* Vol. 17, No. 12, p70-74, December, 1981.

Filas, F., "Three-Dimensional Image Analysis Confirms Pontius Pilate Coin on Shroud of Turin," *News Release.* Loyola University of Chicago, June 11, 1981.

_____, "Second Rare Pontius Pilate Coin Definitively Confirms Previous Coin Imprints on Shroud of Turin," *News Release.* Loyola University of Chicago, November 16, 1981.

Gilbert, R., and Gilbert, M., "Ultraviolet-Visible Reflectance and Fluorescence Spectra of the Shroud of Turin," *Applied Optics.* Vol. 19, No. 12, p1930-1936, June 1980.

Heller, J., and Adler, A., "A Chemical Investigation of the Shroud of Turin," *Can. Soc. Forens, Sci. J.* Vol. 14, No. 3, p81-103, 1981.

McCrone, W., and Skirus, C., "Light Microscopical Study of The Turin Shroud I," *The Microscope.* Vol. 28, No. 3, p105-113, McCrone Research Institute, Chicago, 1980.

McCrone, W., "Light Microscopical Study of the Turin Shroud II," *The Microscope.* Vol. 28, No. 4, p115-128, 1980.

_____, "Microscopical Study of the Turin Shroud III," *The Microscope.* Vol. 29, p19-38, 1980.

Murphy, C., "Shreds of Evidence," *Harper's.* Vol. 263, No. 1578, p42-65, November, 1981.

Pellicori, S., and Evans, M., "The Shroud of Turin Through the Microscope," *Archaelogy.* Vol. 34, No. 1, p34-43, January, 1981.

Pellicori, S., and Chandros, R., "Portable unit permits UV/vis Study of Shroud," *Industrial Research and Development,* p186-189, February 1981.

Pellicori, S., "Spectral Properties of the Shroud of Turin" *Applied Optics,* Vol. 19, No. 12, p1913-1920, June, 1980.

Schwalde, L, and Rogers, R., "The Physics and Chemistry of the Shroud of Turin: A Summary of the 1978 Investigation," *Analytica Chimica Acta*, Amsterdam: Elsevier Scientific Publishing Co., 135 (1982).

Thomas, M., "The Shroud of Turin," *Rolling Stone*. December 28, 1978 - January 11, 1979.

Tyrer, J, "Notes Upon The Turin Shroud as a Textile," Manchester Chamber of Commerce, Manchester.

Weaver, K.F., "The Mystery of the Shroud," *National Geographic*. Vol. 157, No. 6, June, 1980.

INDEX

Abbey of Lirey, 44
Abbott, Rev. Walter, S.J., 55
Abgar V, Archon of Edessa, 24, 26, 39
Academie des Inscriptions, 55
Adler, Alan, 99, 100
Alexius of Comenos, 17
Aloes, Aloetin, 62, 63, 122, 123
Ammoniacal vapors, 63
Anatolia, Turkey, 87, 88
Antonius, Placentinus, 17
Aramaic, 11, 12
Arculph or Arculphus, a French bishop, 17, 38
Avellino, 6
Aymon of Geneva, 33
Ballestrero of Turin, Archbishop, 46, 92, 95
Barbet, Pierre, 39, 65-68, 71 74-76, 78, 80, 92, 100, 109, 114
Basilicas, 38
Berthelot, M., 65
Biblical References
    (John 4:24), 127
    (John 14:8), 127
    (John 19:39), 13, 122, 123
    (John 20:1-10), 119
    (Luke 9:29), 121
    (Luke 22:44), 23
    (Luke 23:53), 13
    (Mark 9:2,3), 121
    (Mark 15:46), 12
    (Mark 17:2), 121
    (Mark 27:57ff), 12
Bithynia, Asia Minor, 38
Blood stains, 63, 64, 100, 118
Borromeo, Charles, Archbishop of Milan, 36
Braulion, St., the Bishop of Saragossa, 17, 38
British Society for the Turin Shroud, 21
Bucklin, Robert, 108, 109, 114
Burden, Annette, 107

Burial Cloth(s), 2, 3, 15, 16, 59, 60, 61, 81, 118
Burial oils, 62, 108, 122
Byzantine icons, 20, 90
Carbon-14 (dating, testing), 90, 101, 102, 127
Carbonate of ammonia, 63
Catacombs, 85
Catalogue (1247), 41
Cathedral of St. John, 7, 95
Cellulose degradation, 101, 106-108, 110-113
Chambery, the capital of Savoy, 35, 46, 51, 105
Chapel des Buessarts, 33
Chevalier, Abbe Ulysse, 54, 55, 57, 58, 59
Chevalier's monograph, 54, 57, 59
Christendom, 5, 24, 25
Christianity, 12, 17, 18, 24, 30, 38, 126
Christian(s), 2, 16, 17, 18, 24, 25, 27
Church of My Lady St. Mary of Blachernae, 27, 41, 43
Clement, 32
Clement V, 40
Clement VII, 33
Clovio, Giulio, 13
Coins, 88-91, 94, 102, 113, 125
Colson, Rene, 62, 63, 122
Constantine Augustus, the Great, 17, 18, 38, 70, 90
Constantinople, 17, 22, 25, 27-30, 40-41, 43, 46, 87, 88
Cottino, Right Reverend Jose, 92
Crown of Thorns, 81
Crucifixion, 2, 23, 72, 74, 79, 80, 125, 126
Crusaders, 27, 28, 29, 30
Daniel-Rops, H., 71
D'Arcis, Peter, Bishop of Troyes, 32, 54
Dead Sea, 5, 87
de Charnay, Geoffrey, 30, 44

de Charny (or de Charney), 8, 30,
  31, 32, 44, 46
de Charny, Margeruite, 33, 44,
  45, 46
De Clari, Robert, 27
Delage, Yves, 58, 59, 61, 63, 64,
  65, 82, 122, 124
DeSalvo, John A., 3, 4, 109-113
  109-113
De Trainel, Garnier, Bishop of
  Troyes, 43
De Vergy, Jeanne, 31, 32, 33
Duke of Aosta, 48
Duke(s) of Savoy, 35, 36, 45, 46
Duomo in Turin, 95
Dyes, experiments with, 61
Eastern Church, 40
Edessa, city of, 23, 25, 26, 39, 40,
  87
Emperor Baldwin, 17
Enrie, Giuseppe, 56, 93
Fake Shrouds, 104
False relics, 32
  pieces of the true cross
  bones of saints
  vials of a saint's blood
Febrile, or morbid, sweat, 63
Fibers, 96, 113
Filas, Father Francis, 89, 102, 113
  113
Fire (1532), 6, 35, 36, 51, 105-107
  112, 113
Flagrum, 69, 70, 73
Flash Theory, 107
Fourth Crusade, 27, 29
Frei, Professor Max, 85, 86, 87,
  88, 96
French Academy of Sciences, Paris,
  64, 65, 82, 122
Gamaliel, 128
Gambescia, Joseph, 79, 100
Geoffrey I, Le Compte de Charny,
  Lord of Champagne, and Grand
  Standard Bearer, 44
Geoffrey II, 32

Geoffrey of Saint-Omer, 28
German, John, 111
Gonella, Luigi, 101
Greek version, 12
Gressman, H., 71
Groton, Connecticut exhibition,
  103, 117
Hagia Sophia, 25
Helena, St., the mother of
  Constantine the Great, 16, 38
Hippolyte sur Doubs, St., 33
Holy Sepulcher, 31
Holy Shroud Guild, 55, 95, 103
Holy Spirit, 123
"Hot statue" theory, 107
House of Savoy, 8, 33, 44, 96
Hugh of Payens, 28
Humbert of Villersexel, 33
Hydropericardial fluid, 78
Iconoclasts, 39
Iconographic theory, 85, 124
Icons, 2, 18, 20, 29, 82, 83, 85, 90
Image formation, 4, 99
Image of Edessa, 20, 21
Infrared-reflectance scans, 96
Institut Catholique, Paris, 59
Interpretation Systems VP-8
  Image Analyzer, 93, 104
Jackson, John P., 93, 94, 104
Janney, Joan, 99, 107
Jehohanan, 76
Jerusalem, 16, 17, 28, 37, 38, 39,
  76, 87
Jesus, 1, 2, 3, 5, 10, 11, 13, 15, 16,
  17, 18, 20, 23, 25, 26, 27, 35, 65,
  72, 74, 82, 83, 88, 89, 117, 118,
  123, 126, 127, 128
Jewish burials, 5
Jewish custom, 13
Jewish law, 69
John Damascene, St., 17
John, St., 15, 16, 79, 80, 119, 120
John the Baptist, 16
John the Good, King, 30, 32, 44

Joseph of Arimathea, 13, 15, 84, 123
Julian, 18
Jumper, Eric, 93, 109, 118
Justinian II, 90
Knights of Malta, 40
Knights of St. John, 40
Knights Templar, Order of, 28, 30, 40, 41
Lactic acid, 3, 111, 112, 113
Lamsa translation, 3, 123
Lirey, France, 8, 11, 21, 30, 32, 37, 44, 45, 46
London, Ron, 107
Loose spices theory, 123
Louis I, Duke of Savoy, 33, 44, 46
Mandylion, 21-27, 29, 40
Mary Magdalene, 119
Mary, the mother of Jesus, 16
Mesarites, Nicholas, 27
Microchemical evaluation, 99
Microfragments, 88
Middle Ages, artists of , 72, 73, 75, 81, 124
Miller, Vernon, 103
Mirabel, 44
Mosaic, 90
Mount Saint Alphonsus Redemptorist Seminary, Esopus, New York, 95
Murphy, Cullen, 94, 96
Musee de Cluny, Paris, 30
Myrrh, 62, 63, 122, 123
Nails, 74-76, 100-102,
Negative image, 50, 54, 61, 62, 73, 84, 85
New London Symposium, 37, 97, 98, 102, 103
Nicephorus, an ecclesiastical historian, 16, 38
Nicodemus, 15, 84, 122, 123
Nineteenth Century, 36, 70
Nino, St., 17
Olive oil, 62, 63, 122, 123
Optical Microscope, 86

Ordericus Vitalis, English monk, 26
Order of Redemptorists, 55
Otterbein, Father Adam, C.ss.R., 55
Our Lady of Lirey, 32
Paint, 60, 61
Painting anomalies, 82, 83, 84
Patibulum, 73, 75
Pellicori, Samuel, 108, 110, 111
Pericardium, 78, 79
Peshitta, 12
Pharos Chapel, 27
Phillip the Fair, King of France, 29, 30, 40, 42, 43, 44
Photography, 47, 49, 56, 100, 103
Photomosaics, 96
Physiochemical phenomenon, 64
Pia, Secondo, 10, 47, 48, 49, 52, 54, 56, 57, 59, 60, 64, 109, 126
Poitiers, 44
Pollen (palynology), 86, 87, 88, 96, 124
Pontius Pilate, Procurator of Judea, 89, 102, 128
Poor Clares, 6, 36, 51
Poor Knights of Christ of the Temple of Solomon, 28
Popes
  Julius II, 35
  Pius, 21
  Pius XI, 50
  Stephen III, 26
Porphyrogenitus, Constantine, 22, 23, 24
Positive image, 49, 52, 66, 109
Princess Clothilde, 48
Queen Anne of Brittany, 35
Reeves, Helen, 3
Resurrection, 3, 107, 109, 114, 117, 118, 123, 126
Reubens, 75, 76
Revised Standard Edition, 12
Revised Vaporgraphic-Direct Contact Hypothesis, 111
Rinaldi, Father Peter M., S.D.B., 95

Rogers, Ray, 94, 99, 105, 107
Romanus Lecapenus, Byzantine Emperor, 22, 25
Royal Chapel, 48
Royal Chapel of the House of Savoy, 6, 8
Sabbath, 15
Sainte Chapelle of the Holy Shroud, Chambery, 35, 51
Saints, see individual names
Sanhedrin, 16, 123
Sarcophagi, Christian, 18
Sardinian Constitution, 45
Saul of Tarsus, 16
Savio, Mons. Pietro, 41
Schwalde, L., 99
Scourging, 68, 69, 70, 81, 125
Shroud of Turin Research Project (STURP), 37, 63, 94, 95, 96, 98, 102, 103, 109, 111, 117, 121, 122, 124
Sindonological Society, 96
Sindonologist(s), 1, 28, 71, 94
Sisters of St. Joseph, 96
Solaro, Rev. Father, 43
Somerset, 29
Sox, David 46
Space of Destot, 74, 74, 76
Spectrophotometer, 110
Symposium of the Shroud of Turin Research Project, 26, 102, 103, 117
Templecombe, village of, 29
Textile Research, 59, 60
Thaddeus, 24
Thermograms, 96
Three-dimensional data, 94, 103, 104, 112, 121, 125
Thurston, Father Herbert, 55
Titus, 39
Topp, Mrs. A., 29
Transmutation, 119
Troyes, Bishop of, 61

Turin's Cathedral of St. John the Baptist (Duomo Giovanni Battista), 6
Turin (Torino), Italy, 5, 8, 36, 39, 46, 47, 56, 59, 95, 96, 97
Tyrer, John, 112
Umberto I, King, 48, 54
Umberto (Humbert) II of Savoy, 8, 45, 92
Van Dyke, 75
Vaporgraph hypothesis, 62, 105, 106, 122, 123
Vatican, 45, 54
Venerable Bede, 17
Vignon, Paul, 11, 20, 43, 44, 57, 59-65, 82-85, 88, 90, 92, 93, 105, 106, 114, 122-125
Villandre, Dr., 80, 81
Vita Photographica Italiana, 56
Volckringer pattern, 109, 110, 111, 112
Walsh, John, 10
Water stains, 53, 113
Weaver, Kenneth, 8
Whanger, Alan D., 90
William of Tyre, Twelfth Century historian, 17
Willibald, St., 17
Wilson, Ian, 21, 22, 23, 24, 26, 28, 37, 40, 46
Woolam, Josie, 39
Wounds, five,
Wounds, 67, 78, 80, 81, 108, 118
Wounds, five,
    On the head, 67, 68, 70, 81
    From scourging, 68, 69, 70, 81
    On the shoulders, 70, 71, 72, 73,
    On the wrist and feet, 73, 74, 75, 76, 81
    On the side, 78, 79
Wuenschel, Father Edward A., 66
X-ray fluorescence spectra, 96